Educational Leadership
Performance Standards, Portfolio Assessment, and the Internship

P. Lená Morgan
C. Jay Hertzog
Albert S. Gibbs

A SCARECROWEDUCATION BOOK

The Scarecrow Press, Inc.
Lanham, Maryland, and London
2002

A SCARECROWEDUCATION BOOK

Published in the United States of America
by Scarecrow Press, Inc.
A Member of the Rowman & Littlefield Publishing Group
4720 Boston Way, Lanham, Maryland 20706
www.scarecroweducation.com

4 Pleydell Gardens, Folkestone
Kent CT20 2DN, England

British Library Cataloguing in Publication Information Available

Library of Congress Cataloging-in-Publication Data
Morgan, P. Lená
  Educational leadership : performance standards, portfolio assessment, and the internship /
P. Lená Morgan, C. Jay Hertzog, Albert S. Gibbs.
    p. cm.
Includes bibliographical references and index.
ISBN 0-8108-4389-3 (pbk. : alk. paper)
ISBN 0-8108-4265-3 (paper : alk. paper)
  1. School administrators—Training of—United States—Handbook, manuals, etc. 2. School
management and organization—Study and teaching (Internship)—United States—Handbooks,
manuals, etc. 3. Interns (Education)—United States—Handbooks, manuals, etc. 4. Internship
programs—United States—Handbooks, manuals, etc.   I. Hertzog, C. Jay., 1946–   II. Gibbs,
Albert S., 1945–   III. Title.
LB1738.5 .M67 2002
371.2'00973—dc21
                                                                                    2001057699

∞ ™ The paper used in this publication meets the minimum requirements of
American National Standard for Information Sciences—Permanence of
Paper for Printed Library Materials, ANSI/NISO Z39.48-1992.
Manufactured in the United States of America.

Contents

〰️ Preface

This manual is intended to serve as a guide for students enrolled in an internship program in educational leadership, their field supervisors, school systems accepting interns, and university supervisors. It should not be considered as a comprehensive statement on the internship program. There most certainly will be program aspects on which all parties will have to confer.

Purposes of the Manual

1. To provide a structure upon which to build a field experience for the leadership intern program. Included within this structure are the following components:
    - An overview of the internship program from its inception and the conceptual framework of an educational leadership program and its component parts.
    - An examination of the National Council for Accreditation of Teacher Education Guidelines for the Internship (1995), the guidelines for the National Policy Board for Educational Administration (1993), and the Interstate School Leaders Licensure Consortium.
    - The roles and responsibilities of the intern, the university, and the school in which the internship will be carried out.
    - An outline of seminars designed address issues not covered in the intern's coursework, such as professional image, the need

for ethics in administration, and a look at the three settings of
administration (elementary, middle, and high school).

- An examination of the various forms of intern assessment, with
  activities designed to synthesize the intern's coursework as it
  relates to the intern experience through coursework and in-
  basket activities.

2. To provide those involved in the educational leadership intern
   program a format for development of the leadership portfolio.
3. To provide a quantitative and qualitative mechanism for evaluation
   of the leadership intern through the use of intern logs, the
   development of the intern's school development project, and the
   completion of the field supervisor's evaluation form.

≈ Acknowledgments

We acknowledge the diligent work of numerous graduate students who share our belief in the need for alternative assessment measures for educational leaders. These students assisted us in making the connection between theory and practice be a reality that could be documented. These graduate students field-tested the assessment methods and the internship model presented in this manual. Four graduate students were willing to allow us to include their leadership narratives in this book: Richard Campbell, Lowndes County School System, Valdosta, Georgia; Beth Checkovich, Frederick County Public Schools, Winchester, Virginia; Richard Fletcher, Shenandoah County Public Schools, Quicksburg, Virginia; and George Kornegay, Thomas County School System, Thomasville, Georgia.

In addition, we would like to thank Mary Anne Gibbs, Tift County School System, Tifton, Georgia, and Susan Yamamoto, Leadership Academy, George Mason University, Fairfax, Virginia, for their comments and advice as we prepared the manuscript. Their advice was invaluable.

Special thanks go to Dr. Virginia Wylie, a career educator, who contributed to chapter 1 and encouraged us to write this book. Also, thanks are due to Dr. Donald Washington for his timely assistance in obtaining some of the necessary references for this manuscript. Finally, we wish to thank our families for their endless encouragement throughout this process.

Section 1
Knowledge Base

The purpose of this section is to review the historical changes that have occurred in internship programs, examine the nature of the internship in educational leadership, and provide a model that demonstrates the role of the internship in educational leadership preparation programs today. In addition, the twelve guidelines adopted by the National Council for Accreditation of Teacher Education (NCATE) in October 1995, which provide the foundation for the internship, are presented. This section also provides corresponding knowledge, a skill base, and performance standards adapted from the National Policy Board for Educational Administration (NPBEA) manual and the Interstate Leadership Licensure Consortium (ISLLC).

Chapter 1
Trends in the Administrative Internship

THE PROBLEM

Today's leadership preparation programs face mandates for change as a result of national, state, and local policies that demand institutional reform and accountability. Accreditation agencies and other professional bodies support these demands with their own guidelines. The America 2000 goals (McKernan, 1994) sum up a growing consensus that school improvement must take place to serve the needs of all the nation's youth and contribute to a better world.

The school leaders in local schools across the country must implement the changes necessary to meet these worthy goals for the future. In turn, universities bear responsibility for providing excellent leadership preparation programs that assist school leaders in performing their increasingly demanding role. Inevitably, all components of leadership preparation programs are under scrutiny and have been under attack in the latest wave of ongoing educational reform (Griffiths, Stout, & Forsyth, 1988).

The administrative internship has been a particular focus of public attention and concern in reform efforts (Peper, 1988). It has become a target of criticism because, first, the university lacks direct control and, second, on account of the various local and state expectations and requirements, the quality of interns' administrative experiences differs from one location to another. In many instances, criticism of the internship has been justified. These concerns should be the point of departure for the review of leadership preparation programs, strengthening them and exploring methods to make the internship the relevant culminating experience it should be and can be for our future school leaders.

HISTORICAL PERSPECTIVE

How the administrative internship came into being and developed through the years into an established component of leadership preparation programs clarifies the problems now faced and also directs educational leaders toward solutions. Before 1900, formal preparation programs for school administrators were rare. Schools were managed by teachers, teachers of teachers, teaching principals, and others who learned on the job. They were hired by local communities as much for their moral character as for any skills they might possess (Campbell, Fleming, Newell, & Bennion, 1987).

Reacting to demands for better prepared school managers to meet the needs of a growing society, the twentieth century ushered in the beginning of the prescriptive era in educational administration (Murphy, 1993a). Practitioners had been criticized for their lack of grounding in the management principles of the corporate world, such as those proposed by Frederick Taylor (Hanson, 1991; Hoy & Miskel, 1991). In response, states began to require formal coursework for administrative positions and to certify graduates of preparation programs for employment. More and more principals and superintendents began their careers with a background of college training.

However, early training for administrators was essentially the same as that for teachers—an assortment of education courses and, inevitably, field study. Thus, the first administrative internships were modeled on that of the student teaching experience in teacher education, and both were originally similar in concept to the old craft apprenticeship (Campbell et al., 1987).

Trends in the administrative internship since the early days have paralleled trends in the development of leadership preparation programs in general. Beginning around 1910, the scientific management movement, followed by the human relations movement of the 1930s and 1940s, particularly as these movements influenced the corporate world, led to changes in administrative preparation programs that persisted into the 1950s (Murphy, 1993a). The primary objective of the new programs was to differentiate training programs for school administrators from those of teachers. This objective was to be accomplished by helping students better understand the specific tasks and responsibilities that comprised the job of administration and to train them to perform successfully in the management roles they would assume.

Course content for administrators continued to be highly technical throughout the prescriptive era, gradually incorporating the new emphasis on human relations in cooperative educational activities. These program components, as part of this new training, became the basis for the traditional administrative internship. The original purpose of the internship was to apply content, presumably taught and learned in the classroom, to a field experience jointly supervised by college-based faculty and senior practitioners. Application was usually observing and participating in how-to activities. Weaknesses in the traditional internship were soon apparent, not only in the typical loose supervision provided but also, more important, because of the nature of the program content itself. Coursework tended to be fragmented and disjointed, and professors paid almost no attention to the conceptual framework of the work of school administrators.

The scholarship of the prescriptive era has been described by Griffiths (1988), Murphy (1993a) and others as naked empiricism and an encyclopedia of facts, resulting in the development of fuzzy concepts that lacked the unifying power of interpretive theories. Typically, a professor of educational administration was a former school superintendent whose course content consisted of personal anecdotes or war stories, folklore and testimonials, and preachments about how administrators should perform. Participants exited administrative preparation programs with little more than a do-as-I-did philosophy.

Calls for improvements brought forth changes in college and university preparation programs. At mid-century the prescriptive era in educational administration gave way to a new scientific era that lasted well into the 1980s (Murphy, 1993a). Prescriptions drawn from practice were soon overshadowed by theoretical material drawn from the social sciences. For example, bureaucratic systems social systems and other theories were studied along with leadership, decision making, and change models with an eye to strengthening the knowledge base of educational administration. Preparation programs emphasized research and theory building to describe and explain task areas and processes. In discussions of theory versus practice, practice was down-graded and denigrated as consisting merely of disjointed and untested principles.

By tradition, the administrative internship retained its place in preparation programs, but it was not considered a high-status experience or even always required. Many internships were seriously limited in scope and all too often were either structured artificially with a set of insignificant and trivial responsibilities or not structured at all, with learning left to chance. New or already overloaded faculty members were the first to be assigned responsibility for these field experiences.

As late as the mid-1980s, the typical internship was often disparaged as an experience of mutual convenience, with little regard for course sequencing, field placement, or the qualifications of either school or university supervisors. According to Richards and Fox (1990), the intern, usually a teacher with a full-time or, at best, a part-time classroom assignment, agreed to devote planning and lunch periods and before and after-school time to perform duties assigned by the principal. Most principals gratefully gave extra duties to anyone willing to do them. This arrangement was an accepted trade-off for the privilege of completing the internship requirement for university degrees and state certification.

The resulting internship experience invariably incorporated control duties, such as bus, lunch, hall, and playground supervision. Usually included were minor responsibilities such as textbook ordering, test monitoring, front desk duty, miscellaneous paperwork, and other cast-off duties that the principal preferred to avoid. These activities may be a necessary part of the job, but interns limited to them were poorly prepared for their first administrative positions. In short, the effective internships initiated by unique educators in unique settings during this scientific era were overshadowed in most leadership preparation programs by the situational constraints, if not outright indifference, of typical internships. Battle-scarred school administrators beleaguered with the difficult issues reflecting a diverse, changing society were probably justified when they complained that their university programs did not prepare them for an administrative position.

NATIONAL SCHOOL REFORM

The public voices the conviction that contemporary school administrators are responsible for the crises in education. These administrators are often seen as incapable or unwilling to solve the array of problems that plague schools of today, the most often cited being violence, lack of discipline, drug abuse, truancy, low standards, poor curriculum, lack of motivation, lack of respect, and discrimination (Elam, Rose, & Gallup, 1994). Because universities are responsible for the preparation of school administrators, it follows that these institutions are blamed for inadequately preparing them. It is commonly believed that universities have neglected their mission to serve society by their lack of attention to the twin themes of equity (i.e., responsiveness to the needs of specific constituencies) and excellence (i.e., responsiveness to the general needs of the country) (Bacharach, 1990).

In the 1980s, a wave of school criticism and calls for reform placed every facet of leadership preparation programs under serious scrutiny, with all program components found wanting. Content was irrelevant; instruction was dull; performance standards were conspicuously absent. Faculties in departments of educational administration were strongly encouraged to evaluate and improve their own programs and warned that if they do not do so someone else will take over the job. Indeed, the "someone else" has already forced many changes by way of centralized federal and state legislation based on recommendations from business-heavy committees. Mandated standards were incorporated into most leadership preparation programs, with varying results (Bacharach, 1990).

The press for leadership-preparation reform at the national and state levels has led us to seek models for guidance in our efforts to make university programs more relevant. Perhaps the worst accusation that can be hurled at educational leadership departments is that their programs are irrelevant, that they do not prepare future school leaders for the difficult task that awaits them. However, before rushing into programmatic changes, it is imperative to determine if relevance can be found in the prescriptive and scientific eras. Questions that need to be asked are: Must the past be discarded to reform and restructure leadership programs? What must be changed and why?

THE NEED FOR CHANGE

America needs a citizenry that knows how to learn in an organized and disciplined fashion, using the best methodologies and technology available today. Individuals need to know how to think and solve problems—and they must be motivated to learn purposefully from school, books, teachers, each other, and all other available resources and experiences. Ensuring that all children learn what they need to know in today's society is a challenge that has never before faced educational institutions in our country.

The ultimate goal of education is to prepare children for their future. Children are the future. The influence of leadership preparation programs has the potential for far-reaching effects on school programs throughout the nation. This influence should be the ultimate goal of these programs. The responsibility of leaders at all levels includes the notion of vision as defined by Bacharach (1990), "the ability to question established and entrenched traditions in light of the big picture, as well as a clear sense of what that big picture is." It is in this realm that the need for change is revealed.

Schlechty (1990), in discussing schools for the twenty-first century, pointed out that important aspects of the big picture can be learned from changes that have occurred in society. For example, Toffler (1980) predicted that the rapidly developing information and communication ages, the electronic era, and the concept of a global village would force radical changes in schools. Others have focused on the grim political, economic, and ideological conditions of the 1990s. These conditions affect the life prospects of a diverse school population and expose a widespread and compelling need for quality education (Tozer, Violas, & Senese, 1995).

As society becomes more technological and information-based, those who have knowledge and know how to use it will have the power to function successfully in the twenty-first century. In this sense, Schlechty (1990) called schools "knowledge-work organizations." Viewing schools in this sense implies a fundamental shift in the way the curriculum is conceived and organized. In effect, the curriculum becomes the raw material for the knowledge-work process. The richer and more diverse the material, the richer the knowledge-work products will be. When students participate actively in the knowledge-work process, they take knowledge and skills embedded in the curriculum and make them their own.

If the assumption is accepted that schools today have problems reflecting societal changes and demands, and that the traditional curriculum can promote only a widening disparity in learning opportunities for today's youth, then the need for change is clear. Program improvement is needed, and this is as true for teacher and administrator training as it is for the public schools. The key to such improvement is effective leadership. At all levels, the role of educational leadership requires the collaboration and combined know-how of thoughtful, purposeful people.

Leadership preparation programs need a united effort in which practicing administrators and university professors alike assume a professional stance. These individuals must recognize themselves as leaders of leaders, as developers of leaders, and as creators of conditions in which other leaders cope and thrive. Schlechty (1990) maintained that leaders in knowledge-work organizations manage by values and results. Such leaders express visions and assess results. His belief that "purpose shapes vision and vision shapes structure" is a recurring theme throughout the remainder of this book.

THE PROFESSIONAL ERA

The recent wave of criticism of school administrators and how they are trained has been far more devastating and comprehensive than that accompanying the prescriptive and scientific eras (Hallinger & Murphy, 1991; Murphy, 1993b). In fact, according to the American Association of Colleges for Teacher Education, "School administrators risk becoming an anachronism if their preparation programs in schools, colleges, and departments of education do not respond to calls for change in preparing them for professional leadership functions" (1988). Such criticism led to what Murphy termed the post-scientific or dialectic era in school administration (1993a). This new era of turmoil has been characterized by a growing sense of professionalism in the educational leadership community. For example, both the American Association of School Administrators (AASA) and the National Council of Professors of Educational Administration (NCPEA) have advocated the movement toward a professional school model in training programs (AASA, 1982; Murphy, 1993b). Such responses suggested that the new era in school administration could well be termed the professional era (Milstein Associates, 1993).

From this vantage point, the University Council for Educational Administration (UCEA), an organization of more than fifty leading universities, conducted a major review of the criticisms and needs of leadership preparation programs. This led to the publication of *Leaders for America's Schools* (UCEA, 1987). In the summary of this work, UCEA cited the need for major changes and called for the reconceptualization of preparation programs. Following this, the National Commission on Excellence in Educational Administration developed a new vision of school-based change that suggested differences in the responsibilities of school leaders as opposed to school managers (Griffiths, Stout & Forsyth, 1988).

These different responsibilities supported the necessity for high-quality performance in schools and high-quality preparation programs in universities. Ensuring such quality will take a collaborative and coordinated effort by school districts, state agencies, professional associations, and others in addition to the university. The major premise of the National Association of Secondary School Principals (NASSP) Consortium for the Performance-Based Preparation of Principals was that only coordinated efforts to prepare and support school administrators at preservice, entry, and succeeding career stages can provide quality control of leadership preparation programs (NASSP, 1992). The National Association of Elementary School Principals (NAESP) supported the notion that study after study had identified areas of knowledge, specific skills, and values that consistently distinguished leaders of effective schools. Therefore, the reasonable assumption is that common purpose and collaboration among formal stakeholders in the teaching-learning process can structure programs to help principals develop these essential understandings, skills, and values (NAESP, 1990).

Despite the consensus about the weaknesses of current preparation programs and the need for change, there is less agreement about alternative models. The most frequent recommendations include an emphasis on values and social context, the perception of leaders with vision and competence, use of technology and newer methodologies in classroom instruction, cooperation between schools and colleges, and recognition of the importance of craft knowledge. The legitimacy of field-based learning experiences, where knowledge and skills can be applied and demonstrated, has been overwhelmingly reaffirmed (Murphy, 1993b).

Such recommendations have led in turn to general agreement on the key components that should be part of restructured entry-level leadership preparation in order to assure and assess high-quality programs. These components have been summarized by NASSP and include (1) generic knowledge and skills of school administration, (2) substantive content related to task areas and processes of administration, (3) identification of role-specific behaviors to be demonstrated in field settings, and (4) procedures for monitoring and assessing attainment and application of knowledge and skills (NASSP, 1992).

It appears that the emerging trend during the professional era is toward ensuring competence through application and demonstration. In *Performance-Based Preparation*, competence was defined as follows:

Competence can be measured only through an accumulation of evidence, over time, that an individual is able to apply knowledge and perform certain functions and skills in ways which are perceived positively by both the individual and his/her audiences. This conceptualization emphasizes reliability (an accumulation of evidence), validity (apply knowledge and perform skills), and legitimacy (in ways which are perceived as being positive. (NASSP, 1985)

Competence thus has a contextual nature. Students must develop in their initial studies knowledge, skills, and values that can then be verified through performance in a field setting. The NASSP definition of competence is an example of the viewpoint of educational leaders who advocate a field-based component in preparation programs.

The stage is now set for the implementation of a new and effective internship program based on a continuously developing knowledge base with educational reform at its center. The Danforth Foundation decided to apply its resources to help universities develop training programs that were more responsive to school districts' leadership needs (Milstein & Associates, 1993). This decision led to the Danforth Programs for the Preparation of School Principals (DPPSP), which by 1992 included twenty-two universities. This organization initiated two studies. The first study was a survey of participating universities to determine ongoing program change efforts; the second study selected five representative programs to serve as models. Model programs included key reform components and had been developed at universities representing different regions of the country. Case studies were prepared and disseminated to some five hundred higher-education institutions that prepare educational administrators across the country (Milstein & Associates, 1993).

In conclusion, examining alternative models and adapting them to meet local needs and settings have become the new thrust and greatest challenge of the professional era in educational administration. The professional era thus involves a decentralization process whereby reflective educators are complementing national goals and centralized mandates for reform by working together to re-create their own leadership preparation programs in their own institutions.

A MODEL FOR TODAY

With the change of presidential leadership in 1992, the America 2000 education goals were retained but given expanded interpretations and focus (McKernan, 1994). New state administrations rapidly moved the impetus for reform to the local and institutional level. State departments of education were reorganized to become more service oriented.

A conceptual framework model is presented in this chapter to depict the relationship of components in a straightforward manner, but in fact there is overlapping that provides reinforcement. The flow of action is dynamic and cyclic, as students complete one program, enter another, and seek jobs. The first component of the model, "entry," contains the admission and individual assessment modes that are handled jointly by the graduate school and the department of educational leadership. Once students have met admission criteria and are accepted into the program, they flow into the second component, "planning." Here advisors are assigned and individual advisement results in a planned program of study for each student.

The third component, "coursework," contains the modes of knowledge, skills, and application that serve as bases for all academic courses under the aegis of leadership, foundations, research, and psychology. This coursework includes six of the seven required leadership courses as well as core courses, and electives. The seventh required leadership course, the administrative internship, is shown alone, indicating the importance field study plays in the M.Ed. program.

"Evaluation," the fourth component, contains the vehicles used to assess the outcomes of completed M.Ed. degree and fifth-year certification programs of study. Exit assessments at this level include successfully completing sixty quarter hours of coursework for the M.Ed. degree and thirty-five quarter hours of coursework for fifth-year certification (the same leadership courses as required for the M.Ed. degree), passing a comprehensive examination, and passing the state-administered teacher certification Test (TCT) in administration and supervision. The final component, "follow-up," includes recommendations for leadership certification, career guidance, assistance in job placement, and survey data collected from program graduates. Follow-up is a combined responsibility of the department, the college of education, and various career placement and research services provided by the University.

The role of the educational leadership (EDL) advisory council is denoted in the conceptual framework as a central body influencing all program components. This council meets as a group twice a year and is comprised of experienced administrators in the local service area who are interested in assisting with the continuing development of the leadership preparation program. Taken as a whole, these administrators form a cadre of practitioners who can be called upon for information from the firing line and with whom cooperation can be established in school improvement projects. Feedback from this council is invaluable

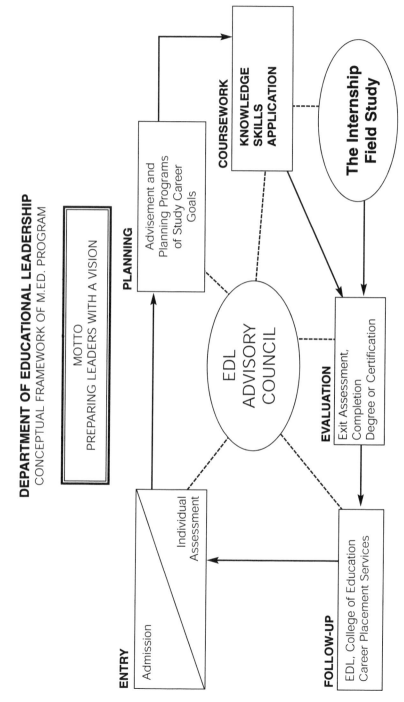

DEPARTMENT OF EDUCATIONAL LEADERSHIP
CONCEPTUAL FRAMEWORK OF M.ED. PROGRAM

MOTTO
PREPARING LEADERS WITH A VISION

PLANNING

Advisement and
Planning Programs
of Study Career
Goals

COURSEWORK

KNOWLEDGE
SKILLS
APPLICATION

**The Internship
Field Study**

EDL
ADVISORY
COUNCIL

EVALUATION

Exit Assessment,
Completion
Degree or Certification

ENTRY

Admission

Individual
Assessment

FOLLOW-UP

EDL, College of Education
Career Placement Services

Legend: --------- **Relationship** ━━━━▶ **Flow of Action**

as a reality check in evaluating course content and methodologies against the problems and needs graduates will face as they assume their own leadership positions.

THE ROLE OF THE ADMINISTRATIVE INTERNSHIP

The internship is the culminating experience at the master's degree level. This interpretation has implications that bear further exploration. Historically, many administrative internship programs were taken by students when convenient and loosely supervised by college faculty. In many cases, the course was available but not required. Students who took it rated it as valuable but not particularly rigorous.

Regardless of various pronouncements, the internship has not generally been understood by either faculty or students to be a theory-into-practice experience in which formal coursework was applied in a field setting. As university supervisors began to realize that a viable leadership preparation program should provide for this application process, program fragmentation had to be addressed. Questions that needed to be answered were: What was the knowledge base totality that students were supposed to apply? What was the purpose of the internship? Decision making would have to be shared by university supervisors, field supervisors, and students. Those who accepted the challenge of the revised internship have enjoyed a sense of involvement in which hard work led to a payoff.

As previously stated, "Purpose shapes vision and vision shapes structure" (Schlechty, 1990). The purpose is school improvement, the vision is leadership, and the structure is based on reason. To promote the teaching-learning process for the benefit of all children, it is the collaborative responsibility of the university, the field supervisors, and the EDL advisory council to prepare school leaders by exposing them to the best available research and theory, to infuse them with a sense of professionalism and competence, and to help them understand how knowledge and skills can be applied with real people, problems, and events.

SUMMARY

In retrospect, it can be seen that the latest educational reform movement has involved strands of influence from the national, state, and local levels, as well as from professional bodies and accreditation agencies. These influences serve as catalysts for change; however, only program-by-program change in institutions of higher education, in collaboration with their constituencies, can bring about valid change in leadership preparation programs. This change requires that individual faculties, working together with field-based professionals, face up to their reason for being and their purpose as professionals. Vision and structure will evolve as reform is undertaken.

Historical trends can provide instructional background. The administrative internship has exemplified every era in the development of leadership preparation programs. Previously, the internship has been thoughtlessly accepted by convention, steeped in trivia, downgraded as the field of educational administration gained a semblance of respectability, and finally recognized as the valuable experience it should and can be. Each era is built upon the successes and failures of the one before, but it is our nature to grow onward and upward. If education is to gain credibility, the time to act is now.

~~ Chapter 2
Educational Leadership
Knowledge and Skills Base

If principals are to meet the educational and developmental needs of their schools, they must continually initiate action and respond to changing conditions. These initiatives and changes are often complex, ranging from implementing new local, state, and federal legislation to resolving explosive family conflicts. Technical skill or reliance on content knowledge alone is insufficient. The heart of professional practice lies between the two poles.

Given the changing nature of the school environment, it is impossible to prepare future educational leaders for every situation they may face. The purpose of this chapter is to provide the administrative candidate with generalizable knowledge and skills to address new situations and traditional patterns. For example, key interpersonal skills such as oral expression and motivating others and core skills such as problem analysis and data-based decision making assist a principal in solving unanticipated problems and in reversing negative developments.

Following a review of states' competency requirements, we selected the National Council for Accreditation of Teacher Education (NCATE) curriculum guidelines for advanced programs in educational leadership for principals, superintendents, curriculum directors, and supervisors, adopted in October 1995, as the foundation for this chapter. These guidelines were formulated through the efforts of the National Policy Board for Educational Administration (NPBEA) to (1) assist in the development of common and higher standards for the state licensure of principals and (2) develop a common set of guidelines for the NCATE accreditation of departments of educational leadership. These guidelines encompass eleven domains, through four broad areas, plus the process domain of the internship. Domains identified constitute the essential repertoire of knowledge and skills required of educational leaders for practice, which are not discrete from one another.

In addition to the NCATE guidelines, knowledge and skills, and performance standards have been adapted from "Principals for Our Changing Schools: Knowledge and Skill Base," which was developed by educational leadership authorities working with the NPBEA. The strategy used to form the knowledge and skills base involved viewing the principalship from two perspectives: inductive and deductive. The outcome of these two processes constitutes the core of what educational leaders must know and be able to do professionally.

The Council of Chief State School Officers, in collaboration with the NPBEA, twenty-four states, and nine associations, crafted a set of standards and indicators for school leaders. The efforts of this group, known as the Interstate School Leaders Licensure Consortium (ISLLC), resulted in a defined set of standards common to all school roles and the incorporation of indicators of performance needed by school leaders in the next century (Van Meter & Murphy, 1998). Provided within this chapter are the six standards and the corresponding performances.

NCATE CURRICULUM GUIDELINES: A SYNOPSIS

Area I. Strategic Leadership

The knowledge, skills, and attributes to identify contexts, develop with others vision and purpose, utilize information, frame problems, exercise leadership processes to achieve common goals, and act ethically for educational communities.

1. Professional and Ethical Leadership: Providing purpose and direction for individuals and groups; shaping school culture and values; facilitating the development of a shared strategic vision for the school; formulating goals and planning change efforts with staff; and setting priorities for one's school in the context of community and district priorities and student and staff needs.

Guidelines

The institution's program prepares school leaders who understand and demonstrate the ability to:

1.1   Facilitate the development and implementation of a shared vision and strategic plan for the school or district that focuses on teaching and learning.

1.2   Understand and create conditions that motivate staff, students, and families to achieve the school's vision.

1.3   Frame, analyze, and resolve problems by using appropriate problem-solving techniques and decision-making skills.

1.4   Initiate, manage, and evaluate change process.

1.5   Identify and critique several theories of leadership and their application to various school environments.

1.6   Act with a reasoned understanding of major historical, philosophical, ethical, social, and economic influences affecting education in a democratic society.

1.7   Manifest a professional code of ethics and values.

2. Information Management and Evaluation: Gathering data, facts, and impressions from a variety of sources about students, parents, staff members, administrators, and community members; seeking knowledge about policies, rules, laws, precedents, or practices; managing the data flow; classifying and organizing information for use in decision making and monitoring. Identifying and evaluating the important elements of a problem situation by analyzing relevant information; framing problems; identifying possible causes; seeking additional needed information; framing and reframing possible solutions; exhibiting conceptual flexibility; assisting others to form reasoned opinions about problems and issues. Determining what diagnostic information is needed about students, staff, and the school environment; examining the extent to which outcomes meet or exceed previously defined standards, goals, or priorities for individuals or groups; drawing inferences for program revisions; interpreting measurements or evaluations for others; relating programs to desired outcomes; developing equivalent measures of competence; designing accountability mechanisms.

Guidelines

The institution's program prepares school leaders who understand and demonstrate the ability to:

2.1   Conduct needs assessment by collecting information on the students, on staff and the school environment, on family and community values, on expectations and priorities, and on national and global conditions affecting schools.

2.2   Use qualitative and quantitative data to inform decisions, to plan and assess school programs, to design accountability systems, to plan for school improvement, and to develop and conduct research.

2.3   Engage staff in an ongoing study of current best practices and relevant research and demographic data, and analyze their implications for school improvement.

2.4   Analyze and interpret educational data, issues, and trends for boards, committees, and other groups, outlining possible actions and their implications.

Area II. Instructional Leadership

The knowledge, skills and attributes to design with others appropriate curricula and instructional programs, to develop learner centered school cultures, to assess outcomes, to provide student personnel services, and to plan with faculty professional development activities aimed at improving instruction.

3. Curriculum, Instruction, Supervision, and the Learning Environment: Understanding major curriculum design models; interpreting school district curricula; initiating needs analyses; planning and implementing with staff a framework for instruction; aligning curriculum with anticipated outcomes; monitoring social and technological developments as they affect curriculum; adjusting content as needs and conditions change. Creating a school culture for learning; envisioning and enabling with others instructional and auxiliary programs for the improvement of teaching and learning; recognizing the developmental needs of students; ensuring appropriate instructional methods; designing positive learning experiences; accommodating differences in cognition and achievement; mobilizing the participation of appropriate people or groups to develop these programs and to establish a positive learning environment.

Guidelines

The institution's program prepares school leaders who understand and demonstrate the ability to:

3.1   Create with teachers, parents, and students a positive school culture that promotes learning.

3.2   Develop collaboratively a learning organization that supports instructional improvement, builds an appropriate curriculum, and incorporates best practice.

3.3   Base curricular decisions on research, applied theory, informed practice, the recommendations of learned societies, and state and federal policies and mandates.

3.4   Design curricula with consideration for philosophical, sociological, and historical foundations; democratic values; and the community's values, goals, social needs, and changing conditions.

3.5   Align curricular goals and objectives with instructional goals and objectives and desired outcomes when developing scope, sequence, balance, and other factors.

3.6   Develop with others curriculum and instruction appropriate for varied teaching and learning styles and specific student needs based on gender, ethnicity, culture, social class, and exceptionalities.

3.7   Utilize a variety of supervisory models to improve teaching and learning.

3.8   Use various staffing patterns, student grouping plans, class scheduling forms, school organizational structures, and facilities design processes to support various teaching strategies and desired student outcomes.

3.9   Assess student progress using a variety of appropriate techniques.

4. Professional Development: Working with faculty and staff to identify professional needs; planning, organizing, and facilitating programs that improve faculty and staff effectiveness and are consistent with institutional goals and needs; supervising individuals and groups; providing feedback on performance; arranging for remedial assistance; engaging faculty and others to plan and participate in recruitment and development activities; and initiating self-development.

Guidelines

The institution's program prepares school leaders who understand and demonstrate the ability to:

4.1   Work with faculty and other stakeholders to identify needs for professional development; to organize, facilitate, and evaluate professional development programs; to integrate district and school priorities; to build faculty as resource; and to ensure that professional development activities focus on improving student outcomes.

4.2   Apply adult learning strategies to professional development, focusing on authentic problems and tasks and utilizing mentoring, coaching, conferencing, and other techniques to ensure that new knowledge and skills are practiced in the workplace.

4.3   Apply effective job analysis procedures, supervisory techniques, and performance appraisal for instructional and noninstructional staff.

4.4   Formulate and implement a self-development plan, endorsing the value of career-long growth and utilizing a variety of resources for continuing professional development.

4.5   Identify and apply appropriate policies, criteria, and processes for the recruitment, selection, induction, compensation, and separation of personnel, with attention to issues of equity and diversity.

4.6   Negotiate and manage effectively collective bargaining or written agreements.

5. Student Personnel Services: Understanding and accommodating student growth and development; providing for student guidance, counseling, and auxiliary services; utilizing and coordinating community organizations; responding to family needs; enlisting the participation of appropriate people and groups to design and conduct these programs and to connect schooling with plans for adult life; planning for a comprehensive program of student activities.

Guidelines

The institution's program prepares school leaders who understand and demonstrate the ability to:

5.1   Apply the principles of student growth and development to the learning environment and the educational program.

5.2   Develop with the counseling and teaching staff a full program of student advisement, counseling, and guidance services.

5.3   Develop and administer policies that provide a safe school environment and promote student health and welfare.

5.4   Address student and family conditions affecting learning by
       collaborating with community agencies to integrate health,
       social, and other services for students.

5.5   Plan and manage activity programs to fulfill student develop-
       mental, social, cultural, athletic, leadership, and scholastic needs,
       working with staff, students, families, and community.

Area III. Organizational Leadership

*The knowledge, skills and attributes to understand and improve the
organization, implement operational plans, manage financial resources,
and apply decentralized management processes and procedures.*

6. Organizational Management: Planning and scheduling one's own
and others' work so that resources are used appropriately and short-
and long-term priorities and goals are met; scheduling flows of activities; establishing procedures to regulate activities; monitoring projects
to meet deadlines; empowering the process in appropriate places.

Guidelines

The institution's program prepares school leaders who understand and
demonstrate the ability to:

6.1   Establish operational plans and processes to accomplish strategic
       goals, utilizing practical applications of organizational theories.

6.2   Apply a systems perspective, viewing schools as interactive
       internal systems operating within external environments.

6.3   Implement appropriate management techniques and group
       processes to define roles, assign functions, delegate effectively,
       and determine accountability for attaining goals.

6.4   Monitor and assess the progress of activities, making adjust-
       ments and formulating new action steps as necessary.

7. Interpersonal Relationships: Recognizing the significance of interpersonal connections in schools; acknowledging the critical value of human

relationships to the satisfaction of personal and professional goals, and to the achievement of organizational purposes; acting with a reasoned understanding of the role of education in a democratic society and in accordance with accepted ethical standards; recognizing philosophical influences in education; reflecting an understanding of American culture, including current social and economic issues related to education.

Guidelines

The institution's program prepares school leaders who understand and demonstrate the ability to:

7.1   Use appropriate interpersonal skills.

7.2   Use appropriate written, verbal, and nonverbal communication in a variety of situations.

7.3   Apply appropriate communications strategies.

7.4   Promote multicultural awareness, gender sensitivity, and racial and ethnic appreciation.

7.5   Apply counseling and mentoring skills, and utilize stress-management and conflict-management techniques.

8. Financial Management and Resource Allocation: Procuring, apportioning, monitoring, accounting for, and evaluating fiscal, human, material, and time resources to reach outcomes that reflect the needs and goals of the school site; planning and developing the budget process with appropriate staff.

Guidelines

The institution's programs prepare school leaders who understand and demonstrate the ability to:

8.1   Identify and analyze the major sources of fiscal and nonfiscal resources for schools and school districts.

8.2   Acquire and manage financial and material assets and capital goods and services, allocating resources according to district or school priorities.

8.3   Develop an efficient budget-planning process that is driven by district and school priorities and involves staff and community.

8.4   Perform budget-management functions including financial
       planning, monitoring, cost control, expenditures accounting,
       and cash flow management.

9. Technology and Information Systems: To be technologically liter-
ate and competent, an educator should have comprehensive skills,
knowledge, and understanding of educational technology to specifi-
cally include audiovisual equipment and peripherals; computer hard-
ware, software, and peripherals; and educational, ethical, and social
issues as they relate to educational technology.

Guidelines

The institution's program prepares school leaders who understand and
demonstrate the ability to:

9.1   Use technology, telecommunications, and information systems
       to enrich curriculum and instruction.

9.2   Apply and assess current technologies for school management
       and business procedures.

9.3   Develop and monitor long-range plans for school and district
       technology and information systems, making informed
       decisions about computer hardware and software and about
       staff development, keeping in mind the impact of technologies
       on student outcomes and school operations.

Area IV. Political and Community Leadership

*These domains reflect the world of ideas and forces within which the
school operates. Explored are the intellectual, ethical, cultural, economic, political, and governmental influences on schools, including traditional and emerging perspectives.*

10. Public Relations: Developing common perceptions about school
issues; interacting with internal and external publics; understanding
and responding skillfully to the electronic and printed news media;
initiating and reporting news through appropriate channels; managing

school reputations; enlisting public participation and support; recognizing and providing for various markets.

Guidelines

The institution's program prepares school leaders who understand and demonstrate the ability to:

10.1 Analyze community and district power structures, and identify major opinion leaders and their relationships to school goals and programs.

10.2 Articulate the district's or school's vision, mission, and priorities to the community and media, and build community support for district or school priorities and programs.

10.3 Communicate effectively with various cultural, ethnic, racial, and special interest groups in the community.

10.4 Involve family and community in appropriate policy development, programs planning, and assessment processes.

10.5 Develop an effective and interactive staff communications plan and public relations program.

10.6 Utilize and respond effectively to electronic and printed news media.

11. Educational Law, Public Policy and Political Systems: Acting in accordance with federal and state constitutional provisions, statutory standards, and regulatory applications; working within local rules, procedures, and directives; recognizing standards of care involving civil and criminal liability for negligence and intentional torts; and administering contracts and financial accounts. Understanding schools as political systems; identifying relationships between public policy and education; recognizing policy issues; examining and affecting policies individually and through professional and public groups; relating policy initiatives to the welfare of students; addressing ethical issues.

Guidelines

The institution's program prepares school leaders who understand and demonstrate the ability to:

11.1 Apply knowledge of federal and state constitutional, statutory, and regulatory provisions and judicial decisions governing education.

11.2 Apply knowledge of common law and contractual requirements and procedures in an educational setting.

11.3 Define and relate the general characteristics of internal and external political systems as they apply to school settings.

11.4 Describe the processes by which federal, state, district, and school site policies are formulated, enacted, implemented, and evaluated, and develop strategies for influencing policy development.

11.5 Make decisions based on the moral and ethical implications of policy options and political strategies.

11.6 Analyze the major philosophical tenets of contemporary intellectual movements and analyze their effect on school contexts.

11.7 Develop appropriate procedures and relationships for working with local governing boards.

Area V. Internship

The internship is defined as the process and product that results from the application in a workplace environment of the strategic, instructional, organizational, and contextual leadership guidelines. When coupled with integrating experiences through related clinics or cohort seminars, the outcome should be a powerful synthesis of knowledge and skills useful to practicing school leaders.

The internship includes a variety of substantial concurrent or capstone experiences in diverse settings planned and guided cooperatively by university and school district personnel for credit hours and conducted in schools and school districts over an extended period of time. The experiences should reflect increasing complexity and responsibility and include some work in private, community, or social service organizations. An optimum internship would be a year-long, full-time experience. Part-time internships for limited periods of time are insufficient.

Participating school districts would be committed to the value of internships and supportive of these guidelines for the internship.

12. Internship: The internship provides significant opportunities in the workplace to synthesize and apply the knowledge, and to practice and develop the skills, identified in the eleven guideline areas. Therefore, the preparation program:

Guidelines

12.1 Requires a variety of substantial in-school and district experiences over an extended period in diverse settings, planned cooperatively and supervised by university and school district personnel.

12.2 Establishes relationships with school leaders acting as trained mentors and clinical professors who guide individuals preparing for school leadership in appropriate in-school and district experiences.

12.3 Includes experiences in social service, private, community organizations.

NATIONAL POLICY BOARD FOR EDUCATIONAL ADMINISTRATION: KNOWLEDGE AND SKILL BASE

Area I: Functional Domains

These domains address the organizational processes and techniques by which the mission of the school is achieved. They provide for the educational program to be realized and allow the institution to function.

Domain 1: Leadership

Providing purpose and direction for individuals and groups; shaping school culture and values; facilitating the development of a shared strategic vision for the school; formulating goals and planning change efforts with staff and setting priorities for one's school in the context of community and district priorities and student and staff needs.

A broad definition of leadership is to shape the quality and character of the institution. A focus of the leadership team as the provider of school purpose and direction provides a narrower definition for leadership.

Performance Standards

1.1   Articulate a personal vision for their school and a well-developed educational philosophy and set high standards for themselves and others.

1.2   Gain insights into a school's culture and school members' personal hopes and dreams.

1.3   Apply knowledge of socioeconomic and educational trends, innovations, and new paradigms to schools and assess how each might affect schools in the future.

1.4   Influence and strengthen school culture by modeling core values, communicating values in symbolic ways, aligning reward systems with values, and selecting and socializing new members.

1.5   Facilitate direction-setting processes within schools that require a high degree of member participation.

1.6   View their schools as a series of systems, as well as a system within a larger system.

1.7   Foster innovation within their schools.

1.8   Facilitate the development of school improvement efforts.

1.9   Utilize the leadership skills of staff and students to plan and implement the change process.

Domain 2: Information Collection

Gathering data, facts, and impressions from a variety of sources about students, parents, staff members, administrators, and community members; seeking knowledge about policies, rules, laws, precedents, and practices; managing the data flow; classifying and organizing information for use in decision making and monitoring.

Information is the manager's main tool for making decisions. The aggregate of information should become knowledge. In summary, information is the gathering or obtaining of facts and/or opinions, followed by their utilization in decision making.

Performance Standards

2.1   Understand information collection as an ongoing process and recognize its importance.

2.2   Perceive the interrelatedness between the information-collection process and the other dimensions of professional practice.

2.3   Diagnose the information-collection needs of their schools.

2.4   Identify various information sources, various strategies for collecting information, and their relative strengths and weaknesses.

2.5   Collect information through multiple modalities.

2.6   Use technologies as well as manual methods to organize and analyze school-based information.

2.7   Summarize and describe information, and present it in written and oral form.

Domain 3: Problem Analysis

Identifying the important elements of a problem situation by analyzing relevant information; framing problems; identifying possible causes; seeking additional needed information; framing and reframing possible

solutions; exhibiting conceptual flexibility; assisting others to form reasoned opinions about problems and issues.

A problem exists in any situation where an individual has no immediate response available that will satisfy the prevailing environmental
contingencies. Thus, recognition of difficulty or disharmony between
the present situation and a preferred state represents a problem for the
educational leader.

Analysis involves breaking the problem into separate parts. Once
the problem has been broken down one, must consider and examine
all of the factors.

Problem analysis involves recognizing a problem and breaking it
down into separate parts before proceeding into problem solving. An
effective educational leader must be able to seek out relevant data and
analyze complex information to determine the important elements of a
problem situation—searching for information with a purpose.

Performance Standards

3.1   Identify problem analysis as a critical step in solving problems
      and as an integral part of the job.

3.2   Analyze work problems in a systematic and logical manner.

3.3   Categorize problems according to general type.

3.4   Describe the relationship of problem formulation to problem
      solution.

3.5   Illustrate the barriers presented by personal behaviors and situ-
      ational factors to problem analysis.

3.6   Describe useful steps for identifying and analyzing information
      related to problems.

3.7   Define connections between hypothesizing and problem analysis.

3.8   Describe the relationship of information synthesis to problem
      solution.

Domain 4: Judgment

Reaching logical conclusions and making high-quality, timely decisions
based on the best available information; exhibiting tactical adaptability;
giving priority to significant issues. Judgment is both the ability to

make good decisions under difficult situations and a process that drives decision making.

Performance Standards

4.1 Identify the core thinking and readiness skills that promote effective judgment.

4.2 Make effective judgments about what is a real or potential problem.

4.3 Identify their weaknesses and enhance their strengths as each relates to core thinking and readiness skills.

4.4 Determine the availability of information to solve problems or to make decisions, and to be alert to new and unexpected information.

4.5 Organize information so that it enhances understanding and recall.

4.6 Judge the reliability, quality and importance of information and ideas.

4.7 Examine information and ideas, and demonstrate an understanding of them as they relate to the big picture.

4.8 Integrate information and ideas in a manner that facilitates effective analysis and evaluation.

4.9 Examine relationships among concepts and ideas to provide a basis for making effective judgments.

4.10 Acquire additional information at a level sufficient to make effective judgments.

4.11 Control emotions so that they do not interfere with effective judgment. use reflection to enhance judgment.

4.12 Make judgments that are morally responsible.

4.13 Develop new ideas using creative strategies.

Domain 5: Oversight

Planning and scheduling one's own and others' work so that resources are used appropriately and short- and long-term priorities and goals are met; scheduling flows of activities; establishing procedures to regulate activities; monitoring projects to meet deadlines; empowering the process in appropriate places.

A major step in organizational oversight is the ability to focus on tomorrow's problems.

After future problems have been identified, the effective educational leader begins planning, planning, planning. Often the planning process is grounded in strategic planning.

Performance Standards

5.1   Work with faculty, parents, students, and other school stake-holders to translate a shared vision into a strategic plan.

5.2   Work with school stakeholders to establish operational plans that support strategic goals.

5.3   Define roles and relationships for implementing and monitoring strategies and operational plans.

5.4   Identify available and needed resources to implement long- and short-range plans.

5.5   Implement global oversight strategies to determine how organizational goals are affected by other goals.

5.6   Initiate appropriate management techniques to implement long- and short-range plans.

5.7   Work collegially with teachers, parents, students, and community to reorder the organization in fundamental ways to make it more responsive to its environment.

5.8   Establish standing plans, policies, standard operating procedures, and rules and regulations that facilitate the implementation and monitoring of strategic and operational plans.

5.9   Develop a pattern of participatory decision making, teamwork, and two-way communication that permeates every aspect and activity of the school organization.

5.10 Build intrinsic rewards into the organizational structure so that students, teachers, parents, and other stakeholders in the school operation are empowered by actions that appropriately support the goals of the school.

5.11 Lead school stakeholders in a holistic evaluation of strategic and operational goals, the resources that have been allocated to achieve those goals, the processes by which those goals have been pursued, and the impact that the pursuit of those goals has had on the organization and its stakeholders.

Domain 6: Implementation

Making things happen; putting programs and change efforts into action; facilitating coordination and collaboration of tasks; establishing project check points and monitoring progress; providing "midcourse" corrections when actual outcomes start to diverge from intended outcomes or when new conditions require adaptation; supporting those responsible for carrying out projects and plans.

Implementation is demonstrated through initiating action and accepting responsibility. To succeed at implementation, one must possess the necessary scheduling, monitoring, coordinating, and reassessment skills. The effective educational leader must be able to shape and reshape plans as necessary.

Performance Standards

6.1 Clarify the roles various staff members will play in the implementation process, what they should expect during the process, and what consequences may result from the actions planned.

6.2 Schedule events and activities that move plans forward.

6.3 Anticipate problems.

6.4 Coordinate activities and encourage collaboration among implementers.

6.5 Monitor project progress.

6.6 Evaluate project outcomes.

6.7 Engage in single-loop and double-loop learning.

6.8 Be supportive of others during a change process.

6.9 reward progress made toward goals.

Domain 7: Delegation

Assigning projects, tasks, and responsibilities together with clear authority to accomplish them in a timely and acceptable manner; utilizing subordinates effectively; following up on delegated activities.

Delegation involves individuals and groups working together to accept responsibility for performing tasks, solving problems, and achieving desired outcomes. An effective educational leader is able to assign new and different tasks or responsibilities to subordinates. Empowerment is a key to successful leadership.

Performance Standards

7.1   Identify the benefits of effective delegations.

7.2   Identify and explain the major elements involved in effective delegation.

7.3   Be aware of potential problems that may hinder delegation and the completion of tasks and projects.

7.4   Use appropriate delegation strategies.

7.5   Display confidence in sharing power or authority with staff— allowing others to make decisions and handle situations on their own.

7.6   Show awareness of assignments, projects, or tasks to be completed, whether delegated or completed by the administrator.

7.7   Communicate and explain clearly to others the assigned responsibilities and expectations.

7.8   Organize delegation efforts so that resources are available to complete tasks.

7.9   Monitor delegatee progress and provide appropriate encouragement and praise.

7.10 Be willing to accept mistakes as part of the learning experience and not criticize others for performing in unique ways.

Area II. Programmatic Domains

These domains focus on the scope and framework of the educational program. They reflect the core technology of schools, instruction, and the related supporting services, developmental activities, and resource base.

Domain 8: Instructional and Learning Environment

Creating a school culture for learning; envisioning and enabling with other instructional and auxiliary programs the improvement of teaching and learning; recognizing the developmental needs of students; ensuring appropriate instructional methods; designing positive learning experiences; accommodating differences in cognition and achievement; mobilizing the participation of appropriate people or groups to develop these programs and to establish a positive learning environment.

Characteristics associated with this domain include the ability to plan, implement, and evaluate instructional programs collaboratively. The effective educational leader possesses an awareness of school curriculum trends, new approaches to organizing schools, state-of-the-art instructional media and methodology, and research on improving student outcomes.

Performance Standards

8.1 Identify the key attributes of skilled instructional leaders.

8.2 Describe the main differences between weak and effective instructional practices.

8.3 Identify the major sources and findings of research on instruction.

8.4 Know how to assist teachers in utilizing reflective practice.

8.5 Describe their responsibility with school staff to set instructional objectives, develop a data base, identify staff development needs, implement desired changes, and evaluate program effectiveness.

8.6 Describe the implications of learning style for instructional design and staff development.

8.7 Identify classroom strategies that respond to various student learning styles.

8.8 Describe the major forms of school scheduling and organizational structures and their relationship to programmatic effects and potential learner outcomes.

8.9 Conduct an exercise in school scheduling or organizational structure with real data.

8.10 explain the relationships among instructional objectives, scheduling, and teaching strategies.

8.11 Identify several current teaching models.

8.12 Understand the principles of measurement and evaluation, including alternative approaches to evaluation and their application to various instructional settings.

8.13 Analyze test data, explain their implications to teachers and lay persons, and link them to school improvement programs.

8.14 Discuss a variety of supervisory techniques and describe their application to teachers in various stages of career development.

8.15 Describe various models of observation and identify ways to ensure their reliability.

8.16 Identify several elements of school culture that support teaching and learning.

8.17 Relate various grouping practices and technological initiatives to desired student outcomes.

8.18 Outline a change process to improve student outcomes.

8.19 Analyze relationships between school plant and instructional programs, and suggest steps to modify a traditional facility to improve the learning environment and faculty collegiality.

8.20 Apply critical pedagogy to three disparate socioeconomic settings.

8.21 Describe several staffing patterns and their relationship to various instructional practices.

8.22 Design a budget process with staff that reflects school priorities for the instructional program.

Domain 9: Curriculum Design

Understanding major curriculum-designing models; interpreting school district curricula; initiating a needs analysis; planning and implementing with staff a framework for instruction; aligning curriculum with anticipated outcomes; monitoring social and technological developments as they affect curriculum; adjusting content as needs and conditions change.

Curriculum includes those courses of study found within a school. The effective educational leader controls the structure of courses of study. In considering curriculum, one must realize that included are course content and the institutional environment in which it is delivered.

Performance Standards

9.1 Describe the curriculum as being broader in scope than courses of study.

9.2 Identify major influences on the curriculum.

9.3 Connect curriculum design to instructional objectives.

9.4 Describe the major movements in American curriculum development, and the assumptions upon which they are based.

9.5 Define the role of principals in curriculum design. define the role of principals in curriculum implementation.

9.6 Define the merits and deficiencies of quantitative and qualitative systems to evaluate curriculum outcomes.

9.7 Define the relationships among curricula, school organization, and society.

9.8 Identify and define the relationships among the written curriculum, the taught curriculum, and the tested curriculum.

9.9 Relate curriculum design and delivery to curriculum management.

9.10 Describe procedures for improving quality control in implementing curricula.

9.11 Describe current trends and issues in several content fields.

9.12 Discuss several curriculum organizational models and the relative merits of each.

9.13 Identify several current curricular issues and their historical antecedents.

9.14 Describe curriculum mapping and its uses.

9.15 Define curriculum alignment and its relationship to curriculum development.

9.16 Analyze several evaluation instruments, and describe their strengths and deficiencies.

9.17 Interpret the selection and use of a variety of assessment tools.

9.18 Describe how schools can use data disaggregation to improve pupil performance.

9.19 Conduct the basic steps involved in needs assessment.

9.20 Involve teachers in the design, development, and management of curriculum.

Domain 10: Guidance

Understanding and accommodating student growth and development; providing for student guidance, counseling, and auxiliary services; utilizing and coordinating community organizations; responding to family needs; enlisting the participation of appropriate people and groups to design and conduct these programs and to connect schooling with plans for adult life; planning for a comprehensive program of student activities.

The principal's key role must be communicated to the stakeholders that student development, guidance, and activities are central to the educational program and must be fully integrated with instruction if students are to fulfill their potential.

Performance Standards

A. Student Growth and Development

   A10.1 Presented with a sample statement of student responsibilities and the associated discipline system, the principal can analyze the document, applying basic principles of human growth and development relevant to student age levels.

A10.2 Presented with part of a sample curriculum, the principal can critique the sample and/or suggest review questions based on basic principles of human growth and development.

A10.3 Presented with a case description of a student with behavior problems, the principal can use basic principles of student growth and development to prepare a set of questions that should be answered before the school takes appropriate action.

A10.4 Presented with a situation involving a faculty member who lacks understanding of the basic principles of student growth and development, the principal can describe an appropriate staff development intervention.

B. Student Guidance and Counseling

B10.1 Given an inquiry from a teacher who wants to know why counselors do not have the same duty roster as teachers, the principal can use basic counseling principles and practices to explain what counselors do with their time.

B10.2 Given an inquiry from a counselor who wants to know why a counselor's presence is needed in the entry areas during student arrival times, the principal can use basic counseling principles to explain the need for the counselor's visibility and interaction with students.

B10.3 Given a student who is having difficulties with his parents, the principal can outline supplemental community resources.

B10.4 Given a school with attendance problems, the principal can draft a plan that involves counseling and instructional staff members and integrates classroom and guidance activities to address the problem.

B10.5 Presented with a challenge by the superintendent and the school board during budget-approval processes, the principal can develop a cogent defense of counseling and its costs.

B10.6   Faced with the need to find a counselor, the principal can develop a job description that outlines the qualifications and duties of the position.

C.   Student Activities

C10.1   In an elementary school, the principal is able to describe how schoolwide student government can be integrated with instructional and management programs.

C10.2   In a middle school, the principal is able to describe the variety of student activities that a typical student population would sponsor during school-time activity periods.

C10.3   In a high school, the principal is able to develop a job description for a student activities director serving the needs of a racially diverse student population.

C10.4   Presented with a case involving the publication of racially sensitive material in the school newspaper, the principal can critique the case using principles of school law and a sample district and school policy.

C10.5   The principal can explain the relationships between student activity and instructional programs and can describe ways to monitor the comprehensive opportunities each provides.

C10.6   The principal an identify criteria by which student activities programs may be evaluated.

Domain 11. Staff Development

Working with faculty and staff to identify professional needs; planning, organizing, and facilitating programs that improve faculty and staff effectiveness and are consistent with institutional goals and needs; supervising individuals and groups; providing feedback on performance; arranging for remedial assistance; engaging faculty and others to plan and participate in recruitment and development activities; initiating self-development.

Purposes of Staff Development: to develop highly qualified personnel, to improve student instruction, to enhance the school mission, to make a personal and meaningful difference for others, to develop positive and productive school cultures, to introduce change.

Performance Standards

11.1 Describe the essential characteristics of a staff development program and the four primary staff development functions.

11.2 Analyze and critique descriptive accounts of successful programs in terms of planning, implementation, and evaluation, and determine if these programs incorporated all of the essential characteristics and primary functions of staff development.

11.3 Demonstrate mentoring, coaching, and conferencing skills.

11.4 Be able to describe the major components of an assessment program designed to evaluate student outcomes.

11.5 Explain the relationship of assessment to strengthening curriculum and instruction.

11.6 Identify the major role expectations for principals in providing assessment programs.

11.7 Examine the data relationships between school goals and student outcomes.

11.8 Draw inferences for revising school programs based on assessment data.

11.9 Design accountability mechanisms based on assessment information.

11.10 Describe the relationship of standards to purposes for evaluating student performance.

11.11 Explain the relationship of assessment to improving student outcomes.

11.12 Identify assessment policies that contribute to the development of sound assessment practices.

11.13 Develop with teachers an outcomes-based, goal-oriented curriculum.

11.14 Describe several specific competencies required of principals in their role as leaders of the site-level assessment program, as managers, and as communicators.

11.15 Explain the relationship of student assessment to school assessment.

11.16 Explain the relationship of assessment at the school site to assessment policies and outcomes at the district, state, and national levels.

11.17 Know how to collect and use needs assessment data on staff development programs.

11.18 Discuss the relationship between staff development and the following: supervision, staff evaluations, the incorporation of new knowledge and skills in classroom practice, and program evaluation.

11.19 Conduct literature searches for each of these items, and identify sources that will keep knowledge and skills up to date.

11.20 Review evaluation studies to identify questions investigated, methods used, principal findings, and the effects of staff development activities.

Domain 12: Measurement and Evaluation

Determining what diagnostic information is needed about students, staff, and the school environment; examining the extent to which outcomes meet or exceed previously defined standards, goals, or priorities for individuals or groups; drawing inferences for program revisions; interpreting measurements or evaluations for others; relating programs to desired outcomes; developing equivalent measures of competence; designing accountability mechanisms.

Measurement is the process of gathering information about students' or staff traits, attributes, or characteristics, whereas evaluation is the comparison of individual (student, teacher, school, system) performance to a particular standard.

Performance Standards

12.1 Describe the major components of an assessment program designed to evaluate student outcomes.

12.2 Explain the relationship of assessment to strengthening curriculum and instruction.

12.3 Identify the major role expectations for principals in providing for assessment programs.

12.4 Examine the data relationships between school goals and student outcomes.

12.5 Draw inferences for revising school programs based on assessment data.

12.6 Design accountability mechanisms based on assessment information.

12.7 Describe the relationship of standards to purposes for evaluating student performance.

12.8 Explain the relationship of assessment to improving student outcomes.

12.9 Identify assessment policies that contribute to the development of sound assessment practices.

12.10 Develop with teachers an outcomes-based, goal-oriented curriculum.

12.11 Describe several specific competencies required of principals in their roles as leaders of the site-level assessment program, as managers, and as communicators.

12.12 Explain the relationship of student assessment to school assessment.

12.13 Evaluate the assessment competencies of teachers.

12.14 Explain the relationship of assessment at the school site to assessment policies and outcomes at the district, state, and national levels.

Domain 13: Resource Allocation

Procuring, apportioning, monitoring, accounting for, and evaluating fiscal, human, material, and time resources to reach outcomes that reflect the needs and goals of the school site; planning and developing the budget process with appropriate staff.

Resources are the available means of supply or support to assist in accomplishing goals and meeting needs. Allocation is apportionment for a specific purpose or to particular persons or things (earmarking).

Performance Standards

13.1 Design resource allocation systems.

13.2 Describe the role of resource allocation in meeting school goals.

13.3 Identify various nontraditional resources available to schools.

13.4 Design a strategy to gain resources from nondistrict sources.

13.5 Describe the relationship of resource procurement to resource appointment.

13.6 design a monitoring and reapportionment system for resource use.

13.7 Develop an accountability system for resource use.

13.8 Connect resource allocation to student outcomes.

13.9 Develop a system for staff participation in determining goals, apportioning resources, and evaluating use of resources.

13.10 Develop and administer a school budget and an activities budget.

13.11 Define resources as human and material as well as fiscal.

13.12 Employ technical procedures such as spreadsheets, planning charts, and program budgeting.

13.13 Develop a school purchasing system.

13.14 Design and administer a materials and equipment inventory system.

Area III. Interpersonal Domains

These domains recognize the significance of interpersonal connections in schools. They acknowledge the critical value of human relationships to the satisfaction of personal and professional goals and to the achievement of organizational purpose.

Domain 14: Motivating Others

Creating conditions that enhance the staff's desire and willingness to focus energy on achieving educational excellence; planning and encouraging participation; facilitating teamwork and collegiality; treating staff as professionals; providing intellectual stimulation; supporting innovation; recognizing and rewarding effective performance; providing feedback, coaching, and guidance; providing needed resources; serving as a role model.

The effective educational leader understands the elements of motivational theory. He or she knows what motivates people and how behavior is initiated, sustained, and discontinued. The educational leader knows that individuals will exert more effort if they believe that doing so will lead to improved performance. Motivation is also dependent upon what an individual expects to get as a result of good performance.

Performance Standards

14.2 Encourage teamwork and collegiality among teachers;

14.3 Articulate the positive impact staff members are having on children.

14.4 Practice participative decision making.

14.5 Be aware of the amount of autonomy various staff members need.

14.6 Encourage close teacher-parent relationships.

14.7 Provide face-to-face and written performance feedback.

14.8 Be aware of various types of feedback systems.

14.9 Understand their impact as role models.

14.10 Enhance individual productivity.

14.11 Articulate performance expectations.

14.12 Be aware of the rewards that staff members value.

14.13 Provide tangible and intangible rewards for good performance.

Domain 15: Sensitivity

Perceiving the needs and concerns of others; dealing tactfully with others; working with others in emotionally stressful situations or in conflict; managing conflict; obtaining feedback; recognizing multicultural differences; relating to people of varying backgrounds.

Sensitivity involves demonstrating consideration toward the feelings, attitudes, needs, and intentions of others and sensing what others feel about themselves and the world.

Expressing sensitivity is more than feeling sensitive.

Performance Standards

15.1   Exhibit behaviors that promote a more positive and caring interpersonal relations climate.

15.2   Use observation skills effectively to gain information about others.

15.3   Choose the physical setting for interactions, and set a tone that reinforces sensitivity regardless of the nature of the meetings.

15.4   Manage conflict by reducing emotions and increasing mutual respect.

15.5   Solicit the perceptions and concerns of others, and seek information from others.

15.6   Recognize achievements and professional contributions.

15.7   Describe the process by which an individual predicts what will occur in a social interaction.

15.8   Illustrate the dynamic and interactive nature of sensitivity.

Domain 16: Oral and Nonverbal Expression

Making oral presentations that are clear and easy to understand; clarifying and restating questions; responding, reviewing, and summarizing for groups; utilizing appropriate communicative aids; being aware of cultural and gender-based norms; adapting for audiences.

Verbal and nonverbal involves language, gestures, and visual cues. An effective educational leader recognizes the importance of sharing of ideas, messages, and attitudes to produce a degree of understanding between the sender and the receiver.

Performance Standards

16.1   Understand, identify, and explain the elements of the communication model.

16.2   Identify effective and ineffective nonwritten behaviors.

16.3   Be sensitive to nonverbal communication behaviors in yourself and others.

16.4   Choose appropriate channels, timing, and settings for intended communications.

16.5 Articulate ideas and beliefs clearly, using proper grammar and word choice.

16.6 Use positive listening skills.

16.7 Send and receive feedback.

16.8 Communicate equally well with teachers, students, parents, peers, district and state personnel, and community members.

16.9 Be aware of cultural and gender factors in communication.

16.10 Be skilled at giving effective presentations to large and small groups.

16.11 Choose appropriate settings for meetings, and make appropriate physical arrangements.

16.12 Use current media technology to enhance and improve communication.

Domain 17: Written Expression

Expressing ideas clearly in writing; writing appropriately for different audiences such as students, teachers, and parents; preparing briefing memoranda, letters, reports, and other job- specific documents.

The Writing Process involves prewriting, drafting, revising, editing, visual appeal, professional imagination, and spell check.

Performance Standards

17.1 Understand the importance of strong writing skills to their careers and schools.

17.2 Assess one's current writing skills and attitudes.

17.3 Understand and apply the four-stage writing process to job-related documents.

17.4 Identify various types of job-specific documents and the functions each serve.

17.5 Produce a variety of well targeted documents that are structurally, grammatically, and technically correct.

17.6 Work cooperatively with others to develop written materials.

17.7 Give and receive feedback on writing skills.

17.8   Use computer technology to enhance and improve the professionalism of written communications.

Area IV. Contextual Domains

These domains reflect the world of ideas and forces within which the school operates. They explore the intellectual, ethical, cultural, economic, political, and governmental influences upon school, including traditional and emerging perspectives.

Domain 18: Philosophical and Cultural Values

Acting with a reasoned understanding of the role of education in a democratic society and in accordance with accepted ethical standards; recognizing philosophical influences in education; reflecting an understanding of American culture, including current social and economic issues related to education.

Philosophy is inherently criticism, having its distinctive position among various modes of criticism in its generality—a criticism of criticisms, as it were. Criticism is discriminating judgment, careful appraisal, and judgments appropriately termed criticism wherever the subject matter of discrimination concerns good or values. The effective educational leader understands that opinions held by different parties about what reality should exist or ought to be like is what makes up democracy in America.

Performance Standards

18.1   Demonstrate critical self-awareness.

18.2   Demonstrate discriminating judgment.

18.3   Demonstrate appraisal of own values and the values of others.

18.4   Demonstrate knowledge of the dialectic of freedom in American education.

18.5   Identify and appreciate the tensions underlying value conflicts in American education.

18.6   Distinguish ought from is, reality and actuality from necessity.

18.7 Identify the diversity of values present in a complex, heterogeneous, and pluralistic democracy.

18.8 Identify the diversity of values in a global society.

18.9 Demonstrate knowledge of the various philosophical perspectives.

18.10 Apply knowledge of philosophical perspectives in analyzing the values in our democracy and global society.

18.11 Know the standard criticisms of each philosophical perspective.

18.12 Understand that reality is socially constructed.

Domain 19: Legal and Regulatory Applications

Acting in accordance with federal and state constitutional provisions, statutory standards, and regulatory applications; working within local rules, procedures, and directives; recognizing standards of care involving civil and criminal liability for negligence and intentional torts; and administering contracts and financial accounts.

Performance Standards

19.1 Demonstrate knowledge of federal constitutional provisions that apply to the public education system by identifying judicially recognized individual rights guaranteed by the First, Fourth, and Fourteenth Amendments to the U.S. Constitution.

19.2 Demonstrate knowledge of federal statutory and regulatory provisions that influence public education.

19.3 Demonstrate knowledge of the state constitutional, statutory, and regulatory provisions that govern a state's educational system.

19.4 Demonstrate knowledge of the standard of care applicable to civil or criminal liability for negligent or intentional acts under a selected state's common law or school code.

19.5 Demonstrate knowledge of principles applicable to the administration of contracts, grants, and financial accounts in a school setting.

Domains 20: Policy and Political Influences

Understanding schools as political systems; identifying relationships between public policy and education; recognizing policy issues; examining and affecting policies individually and through professional and public groups; relating policy initiatives to the welfare of students; addressing ethical issues.

A policy is a purposive course of action, adopted by governmental and organizational actors (or participants) who have the formal authority to make binding decisions. It is manifested in the statutes, regulations, guidelines, and codifications that define the purposes and parameters of specific actions.

An educational leader's political influence is the capacity to affect decisions during the policy-making process.

Performance Standards

20.1   Articulate the general characteristics of political systems and the manner in which those major characteristics apply to school systems.

20.2   Describe the formal relationship between federal, state, local district, and school-site policies.

20.3   Identify the theories of action in an existing or proposed policy.

20.4   Assess the means-end relationships embedded in policies in light of available evidence, and develop conditional recommendations regarding the ability of policy options to attain their stated aims.

20.5   Describe how an existing or proposed policy interacts with other policies and how it complements or challenges the norms and routines of the school.

20.6   Describe how actors in various arenas are (or are not) able to acquire the relative power advantage on particular policy issues.

20.7   Assess the conditions under which prominent political strategies are more or less likely to be effective.

20.8 Develop if-then scenarios that outline alternative political strategies that could be employed to mobilize support for or resistance to particular policy proposals.

20.9 Profile the relationship in the local school setting and indicate how these power relationships affect the likelihood that particular proposals can be enacted and implemented.

20.10 Articulate how policy options affect particular dimensions of quality, equity, efficiency, and liberty.

20.11 Assess policy options and political strategies in light of their moral and ethical implications.

20.12 Assess the political interests and ideals of relevant constituent groups inside and outside the school setting.

20.13 Define and defend the value premises and ethical principles that will guide and govern their behavior in political arenas.

Domain 21: Public Relations

Developing common perceptions about school issues; interacting with internal and external publics; understanding and responding skillfully to electronic and print news media; initiating and reporting news through appropriate channels; managing school reputations; enlisting public participation and support; recognizing and providing for various markets.

An effective educational leader understands that public relations is about building relationships that change attitudes. This cannot occur overnight. An effective public relations program requires sensitivity and careful plan that relies on two-way communication.

Performance Standards

21.1 Construct public relations plans for schools that illustrate knowledge of models.

21.2 Identify a school's internal and external audiences, and design specific messages for each.

21.3 Use mass and interpersonal communications techniques to influence people's attitudes.

21.4 Use one or more techniques to assess a targeted group's level of understanding about a community issue or belief.

21.5 Identify message strategies consistent with the mores of a targeted audience.

21.6 Differentiate between understandable language and educational jargon.

21.7 Define and implement programs in which all school staff are informed of school activities and have an opportunity to provide input.

21.8 Identify the major opinion leaders within their community.

21.9 Understand how to initiate news coverage and respond to reporters' questions.

21.10 Understand the special public relations needs that arise during crisis situations.

21.11 Evaluate communication technologies that would be useful to schools.

INTERSTATE SCHOOL LEADERS LICENSURE CONSORTIUM: STANDARDS FOR SCHOOL LEADERS

Standard 1

A school administrator is an educational leader who promotes the success of all students by facilitating the development, articulation, implementation, and stewardship of a vision of learning that is shared and supported by the school community.

Performances

The administrator facilitates processes and engages in activities ensuring that:

1.1 The vision and mission of the school are effectively communicated to staff, parents, students, and community members.

1.2 The vision and mission are communicated through the use of symbols, ceremonies, stories, and similar activities.

1.3 The core beliefs of the school vision are modeled for all stakeholders.

1.4 The vision is developed with and among stakeholders.

1.5 The contributions of school community members to the realization of the vision are recognized and celebrated.

1.6 Progress toward the vision is communicated to all stakeholders.

1.7 The school community is involved in school improvement efforts.

1.8 The vision shapes the educational programs, plans, and actions.

1.9 An implementation plan is developed in which objectives and strategies to achieve the vision and goals are clearly articulated.

1.10 Assessment data pertaining to students and their families are used to develop the school vision and goals.

1.11 Relevant demographic data pertaining to students and their families are used in developing the school mission and goals.

1.12 Barriers to achieving the vision are identified, clarified, and addressed.

1.13 Needed resources are sought and obtained to support the implementation of the school mission and goals.

1.14 Existing resources are used in support of the school vision and goals.

1.15 The vision, mission, and implementation plans are regularly monitored, evaluated, and revised.

Standard 2

A school administrator is an educational leader who promotes the success of all students by advocating, nurturing, and sustaining a school culture and instructional program conducive to student learning and staff professional growth.

Performances

The administrator facilitates processes and engages in activities ensuring that:

2.1 All individuals are treated with fairness, dignity, and respect.

2.2 Professional development promotes a focus on student learning consistent with the school vision and goals.

2.3 Students and staff feel valued and important.

2.4 The responsibilities and contributions of each individual are acknowledged.

2.5 Barriers to student learning are identified, clarified, and addressed.

2.6 Diversity is considered in developing learning experiences.

2.7 Life long learning is encouraged and modeled.

2.8 There is a culture of high expectations for self, student, and staff performance.

2.9 Technologies are used in teaching and learning.

2.10 Student and staff accomplishments are recognized and celebrated.

2.11 Multiple opportunities to learn are available to all students.

2.12 The school is organized and aligned for success.

2.13 Curricular, cocurricular, and extra-curricular programs are designed, implemented, evaluated, and refined.

2.14 Curriculum decisions are based on research, expertise of teachers, and recommendations of learned societies.

2.15 The school culture and climate are assessed on a regular basis.

2.16 A variety of sources of information is used to make decisions.

2.17 Student learning is assessed using a variety of techniques.

2.18 Multiple information sources regarding performance are used by staff and students.

2.19 A variety of supervisory and evaluation models are employed.

2.20 Pupil personnel programs are developed to meet the needs of students and their families.

Standard 3

A school administrator is an educational leader who promotes the success of all students by ensuring management of the organization, operations, and resources for a safe, efficient, and effective learning environment.

Performances:

The administrator facilitates process and engages in activities ensuring that:

3.1 Knowledge of learning, teaching, and student development is used to inform management decisions.

3.2 Operational procedures are designed and managed to maximize opportunities for successful learning.

3.3 Emerging trends are recognized, studied, and applied as appropriate.

3.4 Operational plans and procedures to achieve the vision and goals of the school are in place.

3.5 Collective bargaining and other contractual agreements related to the school are effectively managed.

3.6 The school plant, equipment, and support systems operate safely, efficiently, and effectively.

3.7 Time is managed to maximize attainment of organizational goals.

3.8   Potential problems and opportunities are identified.

3.9   Problems are confronted and resolved in a timely manner.

3.10 Financial, human, and material resources are aligned to the goals of schools.

3.11 The school acts entrepreneurially to support continuous improvement.

3.12 Organizational systems are regularly monitored and modified as needed.

3.13 Stakeholders are involved in decisions affecting schools.

3.14 Responsibility is shared to maximize ownership and accountability.

3.15 Effective problem-framing and problem-solving skills are used.

3.16 Effective conflict resolution skills are used.

3.17 Effective group-process and consensus-building skills are used.

3.18 Effective communication skills are used.

3.19 There is effective use of technology to manage school operations.

3.20 Fiscal resources of schools are managed responsibly, efficiently, and effectively.

3.21 A safe, clean, and aesthetically pleasing school environment is created and maintained.

3.22 Human resource functions support the attainment of school goals.

3.23 Confidentiality and privacy of school records are maintained.

Standard 4

A school administrator is an educational leader who promotes the success of students by collaborating with families and community members, responding to diverse community interests and needs, and mobilizing community resources.

Performances

The administrator facilitates processes and engages in activities ensuring that:

4.1 High visibility, active involvement, and communication with the larger community are a priority.

4.2 Relationships with community leaders are identified and nurtured.

4.3 Information about family and community concerns, expectations, and need is used regularly.

4.4 There is outreach to different business, religious, political, and service agencies and organizations.

4.5 Credence is given to individuals and groups whose values and opinions may conflict.

4.6 The school and community serve one another as resources.

4.7 Available community resources are secured to help the school solve problems and achieve goals.

4.8 Partnerships are established with area businesses, institutions of higher education, and community groups to strengthen programs and support school goals.

4.9 Community youth and family services are integrated with school programs.

4.10 Community stakeholders are treated equitably.

4.11 Diversity is recognized and valued.

4.12 Effective media relations are developed and maintained.

4.13 A comprehensive program of community relations is established.

4.14 Public resources and funds are used appropriately and wisely.

4.15 Community collaboration is modeled for staff.

4.16 Opportunities for staff to develop collaborative skills are provided.

Standard 5

A school administrator is an educational leader who promotes the success of all students by acting with integrity, fairness, and in an ethical manner.

Performances

The administrator:

5.1   examines personal and professional values.

5.2   Demonstrates a personal and professional code of ethics.

5.3   Demonstrates values, beliefs, and attitudes that inspire others to higher levels of performance.

5.4   Serves as a role model.

5.5   Accepts responsibility for school operations.

5.6   Considers the impact of administrative practices on others.

5.7   Uses the influence of the office to enhance the educational program rather than for personal gain.

5.8   Treats people fairly, equitably, and with dignity and respect.

5.9   Protects the rights and confidentiality of students and staff.

5.10 Demonstrates appreciation for and sensitivity to the diversity in the school community.

5.11 Recognizes and respects the legitimate authority of others.

5.12 Examines and considers the prevailing values of the diverse school community.

5.13 Expects that others in the school community will demonstrate integrity and exercise ethical behavior.

5.14 Opens the school to public scrutiny.

5.15 Fulfills legal and contractual obligations.

5.16 Applies laws and procedures fairly, wisely, and considerately.

Standard 6

A school administrator is an educational leader who promotes the success of all students by understanding, responding to, and influencing the larger political, social, economic, legal, and cultural context.

Performances

The administrator facilitates processes and engages in activities ensuring that:

6.1 The environment in which schools operate is influenced on behalf of students and their families.

6.2 Communication occurs within the school community concerning trends, issues, and potential changes in the environment in which schools operate.

6.3 There is ongoing dialogue with representatives of diverse community groups.

6.4 The school community works within the framework of policies, laws, and regulations enacted by local, state, and federal authorities.

6.5 Public policy is shaped to provide high-quality education for students.

6.6 Lines of communication are developed with decision makers outside the school community.

SUMMARY

An internship program in educational leadership should provide the intern with as many supervisory and administrative experiences as possible. The intern should be prepared to initiate action and respond to changing conditions within the school environment. Reliance on technical skill or content knowledge alone is insufficient.

Adapted from *NCATE Approved Curriculum Guidelines* with permission from NCATE.
Adapted from *Principals for Our Changing Schools* (1993) with permission from NPBEA National Policy Board for Educational Administration.

NCATE, NPBEA, and ISLLC Performance Matrix

NCATE	NPBEA	ISSLC
AREA I. STRATEGIC LEADERSHIP	**Domains 1 & 18**	**Standards 1, 2, 3, 5, & 6**
1. Professional and Ethical Leadership	1.1 Articulate a personal vision for their school and a well-developed educational philosophy, and set high standards for themselves and others.	1.2 The vision and mission are communicated through the use of symbols, ceremonies, stories, and similar activities.
1.1 Facilitate the development and implementation of a shared vision and strategic plan for the school or district that focuses on teaching and learning.	1.2 Gain insights into a school's culture and school members' personal hopes and dreams.	1.3 The core beliefs of the school vision are modeled for all stakeholders.
1.2 Understand and create conditions that motivate staff, students, and families to achieve the school's vision.	1.3 Apply knowledge of socioeconomic and educational trends, innovations, and new paradigms to schools, and assess how each might affect schools in the future.	1.4 A consensus regarding the vision is developed among stakeholders.
1.3 Frame, analyze, and resolve problems using appropriate problem-solving techniques and decision making skills.	1.4 Influence and strengthen school culture by modeling core values, communicating values in symbolic ways, aligning reward systems with values, and selecting and socializing new members.	1.5 The contributions of school community members to the realization of the vision are recognized and celebrated.
1.4 Initiate, manage, and evaluate change process.	1.5 Facilitating direction-setting processes within schools that require a high degree of member participation.	1.6 Progress toward the vision is communicated to all stakeholders.
1.5 Identify and critique several theories of leadership and their application to various school environments.	1.6 View their schools as a series of systems, as well as a system within a larger system.	1.7 The school community is involved in school improvement efforts.
1.6 Act with a reasoned understanding of major historical, philosophical, ethical, social, and economic influences affecting education in a democratic society.	1.7 Foster innovation within their schools.	1.8 The vision shapes the educational programs, plans, and actions.
1.7 Manifest a professional code of ethics and values.	1.8 Facilitate the development of school improvement efforts.	1.9 An implementation plan is developed in which objectives and strategies to achieve the vision and goals are clearly articulated.
	1.9 Utilize the leadership skills of staff and students to plan and implement the change process.	1.12 Barriers to achieving the vision are identified, clarified, and addresses.
	8.16 Identify several elements of school culture that support teaching and learning.	1.15 The vision, mission, and implementation plans are regularly monitored, evaluated, and revised.
	18.1 Demonstrate critical self-awareness.	2.10 Student and staff accomplishments are recognized and celebrated.
	18.2 Demonstrate discriminating judgment.	3.23 Confidentiality and privacy of school records are maintained.
	18.3 Demonstrate appraisal of their own values and the values of others.	5.1 Examines personal and professional values.
	18.6 Distinguish ought from is, reality and actuality from necessity.	5.2 Demonstrates a personal and professional code of ethics.

		5.3 Demonstrates values, beliefs, and attitudes that inspire others to higher levels of performance.
		5.4 Serves as a role model.
		5.5 Accepts responsibility for school operations.
		5.6 Considers the impact of one's administrative practices on others.
		5.7 Uses the influence of the office to enhance the educational program rather than for personal gain.
		5.8 Treats people fairly, equitably, and with dignity and respect.
		5.9 Protects the rights and confidentiality of students and staff.
		5.11 Recognizes and respects the legitimate authority of others.
		5.13 Expects that others in the school community will demonstrate integrity and exercise ethical behavior.
		5.16 Fulfills legal and contractual obligations.
		5.17 Applies laws and procedures fairly, wisely, and considerately.
		6.2 Communication occurs among the school community concerning trends, issues, and potential changes in the environment in which schools operate.
2. Information Management and Evaluation	**Domains 2, 3, 4, 8, 9, & 12**	**Standards 1, 2, 3, 5, & 6**
2.1 Conduct needs assessment by collecting information on the students; on staff and the school environment; on family and community values; on expectations and priorities; and on national and global conditions affecting schools.	2.1 Understand information collection as an ongoing process and recognize its importance.	1.10 Assessment data pertaining to students and their families are used to develop the school vision and goals.
	2.2 Perceive the interrelatedness between the information-collection process and the other dimensions of professional practice.	1.11 Relevant demographic data pertaining to students and their families are used in developing the school mission and goals.
2.2 Use qualitative and quantitative data to inform decisions, to plan and	2.3 Diagnose the information-collection needs of their schools.	2.3 Students and staff feel valued and important.

2.3	assess school programs, to design accountability systems, to plan for school improvement, and to develop and conduct research.	2.4	Identify various information sources, various strategies for collecting information, and their relative strengths and weaknesses.	
2.3	Engage staff in an ongoing study of current best practices and relevant research and demographic data, and analyze their implications for school improvement.	2.5	Collect information through multiple modalities.	
2.4	Analyze and interpret educational data, issues, and trends for boards, committees, and other groups, outlining possible actions and their implications.	2.7	Summarize and describe information and present it in written and oral form.	
		3.1	Identify problem analysis as a critical step in solving problems and as an integral part of their jobs.	
		3.2	Analyze work problems in a systematic and logical manner.	
		3.3	Categorize problems according to general type.	
		3.4	Describe the relationship of problem formulation to problem solution.	
		3.5	Illustrate the barriers presented by personal behaviors and situational factors to problem analysis.	
		3.6	Describe useful steps for identifying and analyzing information related to problems.	
		3.7	Define connections between hypothesizing and problem analysis.	
		3.8	Describe the relationship of information synthesis to problem solution.	
		4.1	Identify the core thinking and readiness skills that promote effective judgment.	
		4.2	Make effective judgments about what is a real or potential problem.	
		4.3	Identify their weaknesses and enhance their strengths as each relates to core thinking and readiness skills.	
		4.4	Determine the availability of information to solve problems or to make decisions, and be alert to new and unexpected information.	
		4.5	Organize information so that it enhances understanding and recall.	
		4.6	Judge the reliability, quality, and importance of information and ideas.	
		4.7	Examine information and ideas and demonstrate an understanding of them as they relate to the big picture.	

2.8	There is a culture of high expectations for self, student, and staff performance.
2.15	The school culture and climate are assessed on a regular basis.
2.16	A variety of information sources are used to make decisions.
2.18	Multiple sources of information regarding performance are used by staff and students.
3.11	The school acts entrepreneurily to support continuous improvement.
5.12	Examines and considers the prevailing values of the diverse school community.
6.1	The environment in which schools operate is influenced on behalf of students and their families.

4.8	Integrate information and ideas in a manner that facilitates effective analysis and evaluation.
4.9	Examine relationships among concepts and ideas to provide a basis for making effective judgments.
4.10	Acquire additional information at a level sufficient to make effective judgments.
4.11	Control emotions so that they do not interfere with effective judgment; use reflection to enhance judgment.
4.12	Make judgments that are morally responsible.
4.13	Develop new ideas using creative strategies.
8.13	Analyze test data, explain their implications to teachers and laypersons, and link them to school improvement programs.
9.16	Analyze several evaluation instruments, and describe strengths and deficiencies.
9.17	Interpret the selection and use of a variety of assessment tools.
9.18	Describe how schools can use data disaggregation to improve pupil performance.
9.19	Conduct the basic steps involved in needs assessment.
9.20	Involve teachers in the design, development, and management of curriculum.
12.1	Describe the major components of an assessment program designed to evaluate student outcomes.
12.2	Explain the relationship of assessment to strengthening curriculum and instruction.
12.3	Identify the major role expectations for principals in providing for assessment programs.
12.4	Examine the data relationships between school goals and student outcomes.
12.5	Draw inferences for revising school programs based on assessment data.
12.6	Design accountability mechanisms based on assessment information.
12.7	Describe the relationship of standards to purposes for evaluating student performance.

12.8 Explain the relationship of assessment to improving student outcomes.

12.9 Identify assessment policies that contribute to the development of sound assessment practices.

12.10 Develop with teachers an outcomes-based, goal-oriented curriculum.

12.11 Describe several specific competencies required of principals in their role as leaders of the site-level assessment program, as managers, and as communicators.

12.12 Explain the relationship of student assessment to school assessment.

12.13 Explain the relationship of assessment at the school site to assessment policies and outcomes at the district, state, and national levels.

AREA II. INSTRUCTIONAL LEADERSHIP

3. Curriculum, Instruction, Supervision, and the Learning Environment

3.1 Create with teachers, parents and students a positive school culture that promotes learning;

3.2 Develop collaboratively a learning organization that supports instructional improvement, builds an appropriate curriculum, and incorporates best practice.

3.3 Base curricular decisions on research, applied theory, informed practice, the recommendations of learned societies, and state and federal policies and mandates.

3.4 Design curricula with consideration for philosophical, sociological, and historical foundations, democratic values, and the community's values, goals, social needs, and changing conditions.

Domains 8 & 9

8.1 Identify the key attributes of skilled instructional leaders.

8.2 Describe the main differences between weak and effective instructional practices.

8.3 Identify the major sources and findings of research on instruction.

8.4 Know how to assist teachers in utilizing reflective practice;

8.5 Describe their responsibility with school staff to set instructional objectives, develop a data base, identify staff development needs, implement desired changes, and evaluate program effectiveness.

8.6 Describe the implications of learning style for instructional design and staff development.

8.7 Identify classroom strategies that respond to various student learning styles.

8.8 Describe the major forms of school scheduling and their relationship to programmatic effects and potential learner outcomes.

Standard 2

2.4 The responsibilities and contributions of each individual are acknowledged.

2.5 Barriers to student learning are identified, clarified, and addressed.

2.11 Multiple opportunities to learn are available to all students.

2.12 The school is organized and aligned for success.

2.13 Curricular programs are designed, implemented, evaluated, and refined.

2.14 Curriculum decisions are based on research, expertise of teachers, and the recommendations of learned societies.

2.17 Student learning is assessed using a variety of techniques.

2.19 A variety of supervisory and evaluation models are employed.

3.5	Align curricular goals and objectives with instructional goals and objectives and desired outcomes when developing scope, sequence, balance, and other factors.
3.6	Develop with others curriculum and instruction appropriate for varied teaching and learning styles and specific student needs based on gender, ethnicity, culture, social class, and exceptionalities.
3.7	Utilize a variety of supervisory models to improve teaching and learning.
3.8	Use various staffing patterns, student grouping plans, class scheduling forms, school organizational structures, and facilities design processes to support various teaching strategies and desired student outcomes.
3.9	Assess student progress using a variety of appropriate techniques.
8.9	Conduct an exercise in school scheduling or organizational structure with real data.
8.10	Explain the relationships among instructional objectives, scheduling, and teaching strategies.
8.11	Identify several current teaching models.
8.12	Understand the principles of measurement and evaluation, including alternative approaches to evaluation and their application to various instructional settings.
8.14	Discuss a variety of supervisory techniques and describe their application to teachers in various stages of career development.
8.15	Describe various models of observation and identify ways to ensure their reliability.
8.17	Relate various grouping practices and technological initiatives to desired student outcomes.
8.18	Outline a change process to improve student outcomes.
8.19	Analyze relationships between school plant and instructional programs and suggest steps to modify a traditional facility to improve the learning environment and faculty collegiality.
8.20	Apply critical pedagogy to three disparate socioeconomic settings.
8.21	Describe several staffing patterns and their relationship to various instructional practices.
9.1	Describe the curriculum as being broader in scope than courses of study.
9.2	Identify major influences on the curriculum.
9.3	Connect curriculum design to instructional objectives.
9.4	Describe the major movements in American curriculum development and the assumptions upon which they are based.
9.5	Define the role of principals in curriculum design. define the role of principals in curriculum implementation.
9.6	Define the merits and deficiencies of quantitative and qualitative evaluation systems to evaluate curriculum outcomes.

9.7 Define the relationships among curricula, school organization, and society.	
9.8 Identify and define the relationships among the written curriculum, the taught curriculum, and the tested curriculum.	
9.9 Relate curriculum design and delivery to curriculum management.	
9.10 Describe procedures for improving quality control in implementing curricula.	
9.11 Describe current trends and issues in several content fields.	
9.12 Discuss several curriculum organizational models and the relative merits of each.	
913 Identify several current curricular issues and their historical antecedents.	
9.14 Describe curriculum mapping and its uses.	
9.15 Define curriculum alignment and its relationship to curriculum development.	

4. Professional Development

4.1 Work with faculty and other stakeholders to identify needs for professional development; to organize, facilitate, and evaluate professional development programs; to integrate district and school priorities; to build faculty as resource; and to ensure that professional development activities focus on improving student outcomes.

4.2 Apply adult learning strategies to professional development, focusing on authentic problems and tasks and utilizing mentoring, coaching, conferencing, and other techniques to ensure that new knowledge and skills are practiced in the workplace.

Domain 11

11.1 Describe the essential characteristics of a staff development program and the four primary staff development functions.

11.2 Analyze and critique descriptive accounts of successful programs in terms of planning, implementation, and evaluation, and determine if these programs incorporated all of the essential characteristics and primary functions of staff development.

11.3 Demonstrate mentoring, coaching, and conferencing skills.

11.4 Be knowledgeable of action research methods as they relate to the investigation and resolution of classroom and school problems.

11.5 Know how to collect and use needs assessment data on staff development programs.

11.6 Discuss the relationship between staff development and the following: supervision, staff evaluations, the

Standards 2, 3, & 4

2.2 Professional development promotes a focus on student learning consistent with the school vision and goals.

2.7 Life-long learning is encouraged and modeled.

3.5 Collective bargaining and other contractual agreements related to the school are effectively managed.

3.22 Human resource functions support the attainment of school goals.

4.16 Opportunities for staff to develop collaborative skills are provided.

incorporation of new knowledge and skills in classroom practice, and program evaluation.

11.7 Conduct literature searches for each of the items above, and identify sources that will keep knowledge and skills up to date.

11.8 Review evaluation studies to identify questions investigated, methods used, principal findings, and the effects of staff development activities.

4.3 Apply effective job analysis procedures, supervisory techniques, and performance appraisal for instructional and noninstructional staff.

4.4 Formulate and implement a self-development plan, endorsing the value of career-long growth and utilizing a variety of resources for continuing professional development.

4.5 Identify and apply appropriate policies, criteria, and processes for the recruitment, selection, induction, compensation, and separation of personnel, with attention to issues of equity and diversity.

4.6 Negotiate and manage effectively collective bargaining or written agreements.

5. Student Personnel Services

5.1 Apply the principles of student growth and development to the learning environment and the educational program.

5.2 Develop with the counseling and teaching staff a full program of student advisement, counseling, and guidance services.

5.3 Develop and administer policies that provide a safe school environment and promote student health and welfare.

5.4 Address student and family conditions affecting learning by collaborating with community

Standards 2, 3, & 4

2.20 Pupil personnel programs are developed to meet the needs of students and their families.

3.21 A safe, clean, and aesthetically pleasing school environment is created and maintained.

4.9 Community youth and family services are integrated with school programs.

Domain 10

A10.1 Presented with a sample statement of student responsibilities and associated discipline system, the principal can analyze the document applying basic principles of human growth and development relevant to student age levels.

A10.2 Presented with part of a sample curriculum, the principal can critique the sample and/or suggest review questions based on basic principles of human growth and development.

A10.3 Presented with a case description of a student with behavior problems, the principal can use basic principles of student growth and development to prepare a set of questions that should be answered before the school takes appropriate action.

A10.4 Presented with a situation involving a faculty member who lacks understanding of the basic principles of agencies to integrate health, social, and other services for students.

5.5 Plan and manage activity programs to fulfill student developmental, social, cultural, athletic, leadership, and scholastic needs; working with staff, students, families, and community.

student growth and development, the principal can describe an appropriate staff development intervention.

B10.1 Given an inquiry from a teacher who wants to know why counselors do not have the same duty roster as teachers, the principal can use basic counseling principles and practices to explain what counselors do with their time.

B10.2 Given an inquiry from a counselor who wants to know why his or her presence is needed in the entry areas during student arrival times, the principal can use basic counseling principles to explain the need for the counselor's visibility and interaction with students.

B10.3 Given a student who is having difficulties with his parents, the principal can outline supplemental community resources.

B10.4 Given a school with attendance problems, the principal can draft a plan that involves counseling and instructional staff members and integrates classroom and guidance activities to address the problem.

B10.5 Presented with a challenge by the superintendent and the school board during budget approval processes, the principal can develop a cogent defense of counseling and its costs.

B10.6 Faced with the need to find a counselor, the principal can develop a job description that outlines the qualifications and duties of the position.

C10.1 An elementary school principal is able to describe how school wide student government can be integrated with instructional and management programs.

C10.2 A middle school principal is able to describe the variety of student activities that a typical student population would sponsor during school-time activity periods.

C10.3 A high school principal is able to develop a job description for a student activities director serving the needs of a racially diverse student population.

C10.4 Presented with a case involving the publication of racially sensitive material in the school newspaper, the principal can critique the case using principles of school law and a sample district and school policy.

C10.5 Can explain the relationships between student activity and instructional programs and can describe ways to monitor the comprehensive opportunities each provides.

C10.6 Can identify criteria by which student activities programs may be evaluated.

AREA III. ORGANIZATIONAL LEADERSHIP

6. Organizational Management

6.1 Establish operational plans and processes to accomplish strategic goals, utilizing practical applications of organizational theories.

6.2 Apply a systems perspective, viewing schools as interactive internal systems operating within external environments.

6.3 Implement appropriate management techniques and group processes to define roles, assign functions, delegate effectively, and determine accountability for attaining goals.

6.4 Monitor and assess the progress of activities, making adjustments and formulating new action steps as necessary.

Domains 5, 6, 7, & 18

5.2 Work with school stakeholders to establish operational plans that support strategic goals.

5.3 Define roles and relationships for implementing and monitoring strategies and operational plans.

5.4 Identify available and needed resources to implement long- and short-range plans.

5.5 Implement global oversight strategies to determine how organizational goals are affected by other goals.

5.6 Initiate appropriate management techniques to implement long- and short-range plans.

5.7 Work collegially with teachers, parents, students, and community to reorder the organization in fundamental ways to make it more responsive to its environment.

5.8 Establish standing plans, policies, standard operating procedures, and rules and regulations that facilitate the implementation and monitoring of strategic and operational plans.

5.10 Build intrinsic rewards into the organization structure so that students, teachers, parents, and other stakeholders in the school operation are empowered by actions that appropriately support the goals of the school; and

5.11 Lead school stakeholders in a holistic evaluation of strategic and operational goals, the resources that

Standard 3

3.1 Knowledge of learning, teaching, and student development is used to inform management decisions.

3.2 Operational procedures are designed and managed to maximize opportunities for successful learning.

3.3 Emerging trends are recognized, studied, and applied as appropriate.

3.4 Operational plans and procedures to achieve the vision and goals of the school are in place.

3.7 Time is managed to maximize attainment of organizational goals.

3.8 Potential problems and opportunities are identified.

3.9 Problems are confronted and resolved in a timely manner.

3.12 Organizational systems are regularly monitored and modified as needed.

3.14 Responsibility is shared to maximize ownership and accountability.

3.15 Effective problem-framing and problem-solving skills are used.

6.1 have been allocated to achieve those goals, the processes by which those goals have been pursued, and the impact that the pursuit of those goals has had on the organization and its stakeholders.

Clarify the roles various staff members will play in the implementation process, what they should expect during the process, and what consequences may occur as a result of the actions planned.

6.2 Schedule events and activities that move plans forward.

6.3 Anticipate problems.

6.4 Coordinate activities and encourage collaboration among implementers.

6.5 Monitor project progress.

6.6 Evaluate project outcomes.

6.7 Engage in single-loop and double-loop learning.

6.8 Be supportive of others during a change process.

6.8 Reward progress made toward goals.

7.1 Identify the benefits of effective delegations.

7.2 Identify and explain the major elements involved in effective delegation.

7.3 Be aware of potential problems that may hinder the delegation and completion of tasks and projects.

7.4 Use appropriate delegation strategies.

7.5 Display confidence in sharing power or authority with staff—allowing others to make decisions and handle situations on their own.

7.6 Show awareness of assignments, projects, or tasks to be completed, whether delegated or completed by the administrator.

7.8 Organize delegation efforts so that resources are available to complete tasks.

7.9 Monitor delegatee progress and provide appropriate encouragement and praise.

18.7 Identify the diversity of values present in a complex, heterogeneous, and pluralistic democracy.

18.8 Identify the diversity of values in a global society.

7. Interpersonal Relationships	Domains 5, 7, 15, 16, & 17	Standards 2, 3, 4, & 5
7.1 Use appropriate interpersonal skills.	5.9 Develop a pattern of participatory decision making, teamwork, and two-way communication that permeates every aspect and activity of the school organization.	2.1 All individuals are treated with fairness, dignity, and respect.
7.2 Use appropriate written, verbal, and nonverbal communication in a variety of situations.		2.6 Diversity is considered in developing learning experiences.
7.3 Apply appropriate communications strategies.	7.7 Communicate and explain clearly to others assigned responsibilities and expectations.	3.16 Effective conflict-resolution skills are used.
7.4 Promote multicultural awareness, gender sensitivity, and racial and ethnic appreciation.	7.10 Be willing to accept mistakes as part of the learning experience and not criticize others for performing in unique ways.	3.17 Effective group-process and consensus-building skills are used.
7.5 Apply counseling and mentoring skills, and utilize stress-management and conflict-management techniques.	15.1 Exhibit behaviors that promote a more positive and caring interpersonal relations climate.	3.18 Effective communication skills are used.
	15.2 Use observation skills effectively to gain information about others.	4.10 Community stakeholders are treated equitably.
	15.3 Choose the physical setting for interactions, and set a tone that reinforces sensitivity regardless of the nature of the meetings.	4.11 Diversity is recognized and valued.
	15.4 Manage conflict by reducing emotions and increasing mutual respect.	5.10 Demonstrates appreciation for and sensitivity to the diversity in the school community.
	15.5 Solicit the perceptions and concerns of others, and seek information from others.	
	15.6 Recognize achievements and professional contributions.	
	15.7 Describe the process by which an individual predicts what will occur in a social interaction.	
	15.8 Illustrate the dynamic and interactive nature of sensitivity.	
	16.1 Understand, identify, and explain the elements of the communication model.	
	16.2 Identify effective and ineffective nonwritten behaviors.	
	16.3 Be sensitive to nonverbal communication behaviors in yourself and others.	
	16.4 Choose appropriate channels, timing, and settings for intended communications.	
	16.5 Articulate ideas and beliefs clearly, using proper grammar and word choice.	
	16.6 Use positive listening skills.	

	16.7 Send and receive feedback.	**Standards 1, 3, & 4**
	16.8 Communicate equally well with teachers, students, parents, peers, district and state personnel, and community members.	1.13 Needed resources are sought and obtained to support the implementation of the school mission and goals.
	16.9 Be aware of cultural and gender factors in communication.	1.14 Existing resources are used in support of the school vision and goals.
	16.10 Be skilled at giving effective presentations to large and small groups.	3.6 The school plant, equipment, and support systems operate safely, efficiently, and effectively.
	16.11 Choose appropriate settings for meetings, and make appropriate physical arrangements.	3.10 Financial, human, and material resources are aligned to the goals of schools.
	16.12 Use current media technology to enhance and improve communication.	
	17.1 Understand the importance of strong writing skills to careers and schools.	
	17.2 Assess one's current writing skills and attitudes.	
	17.3 Understand and apply the four-stage writing process to job-related documents.	
	17.4 Identify various types of job-specific documents and the functions each serve.	
	17.5 Produce a variety of well-targeted documents that are structurally, grammatically, and technically correct.	
	17.6 Work cooperatively with others to develop written materials.	
	17.7 Give and receive feedback on writing skills.	
	17.8 Use computer technology to enhance and improve the professionalism of written communications.	
8. Financial Management and Resource Allocation	**Domains 8 & 13**	
8.1 Identify and analyze the major sources of fiscal and nonfiscal resources for schools and school districts.	8.22 Design a budget process with staff that reflects school priorities for the instructional program.	
	13.1 Design resource allocation systems.	
	13.2 Describe the role of resource allocation in meeting school goals.	
8.2 Acquire and manage financial and material assets and capital goods and services, allocating resources according to district or school priorities.	13.3 Identify various nontraditional resources available to schools.	
	13.4 Design a strategy to gain resources from nondistrict sources.	

8.3 Develop an efficient budget-planning process that is driven by district and school priorities and involves staff and community.	13.5 Describe the relationship of resource procurement to resource appointment.	3.20 Fiscal resources of school are managed responsibly, efficiently, and effectively.
8.4 Perform budget-management functions including financial planning, monitoring, cost control, expenditures accounting, and cash flow management.	13.6 Design a monitoring and reapportionment system for resource use.	4.7 Available community resources are secured to help the school solve problems and achieve goals.
	13.7 Develop an accountability system for resource use.	4.14 Public resources and funds are used appropriately and wisely.
	13.8 Connect resource allocation to student outcomes.	
	13.9 Develop a system for staff participation in determining goals, apportioning resources, and evaluating use of resources.	
	13.10 Develop and administer a school budget and an activities budget.	
	13.11 Define resources as human and material as well as fiscal.	
	13.12 Employ technical procedures such as spreadsheets, planning charts, and program budgeting.	
	13.13 Develop a school purchasing system.	
	13.14 Design and administer a materials and equipment inventory system.	
9. Technology and Information Systems	**Domains 2 & 21**	**Standard 3**
9.1 Use technology, telecommunications, and information systems to enrich curriculum and instruction.	2.6 Use technologies as well as manual methods to organize and analyze school-based information.	3.19 There is effective use of technology to manage school operations.
9.2 Apply and assess current technologies for school management and business procedures.	21.11 Evaluate communication technologies that would be useful to their schools.	
9.3 Develop and monitor long-range plans for school and district technology and information systems, making informed decisions about computer hardware and software, and about staff development, keeping in mind to the impact of technologies on student outcomes and school operations.		

AREA IV. POLITICAL AND COMMUNITY LEADERSHIP

Public Relations Guidelines	**Domains 5 & 21**	**Standards 1, 3, 4, 5, & 6**
10.		
10.1 Analyze community and district power structures, and identify major opinion leaders and their relationships to school goals and programs.	5.1 Work with faculty, parents, students, and other school stakeholders to translate a shared vision into a strategic plan.	1.1 The vision and mission of the school are effectively communicated to staff, parents, students, and community members.
10.2 Articulate the district's or school's vision, mission, and priorities to the community and media, and build community support for district or school priorities and programs.	21.1 Construct public relations plans for their schools that illustrate knowledge of models.	3.13 Stakeholders are involved in decisions affecting schools.
	21.2 Identify the school's internal and external audiences, and design specific messages for each.	4.1 High visibility, active involvement, and communication with the larger community are a priority.
10.3 Communicate effectively with various cultural, ethnic, racial, and special interest groups in the community.	21.3 Use mass and interpersonal communications techniques to influence people's attitudes.	4.2 Relationships with community leaders are identified and nurtured.
	21.4 Use one or more techniques to assess a targeted group's level of understanding about a community issue or belief.	4.3 Information about family and community concerns, expectations, and needs is used regularly.
10.4 Involve family and community in appropriate policy development, programs planning, and assessment processes.	21.5 Identify message strategies consistent with the mores of a targeted audience.	4.4 There is outreach to different business, religious, political, and service agencies and organizations.
	21.6 Differentiate between understandable language and educational jargon.	4.5 Credence is given to individuals and groups whose values and opinions may conflict.
10.5 Develop an effective and interactive staff communications plan and public relations program.	21.7 Define and implement programs in which all school staff are informed of school activities and have an opportunity to provide input.	4.6 The school and community serve one another as resources.
	21.8 Identify the major opinion leaders within their community.	4.8 Partnerships are established with area businesses, institutions of higher education, and community groups to strengthen programs and support school goals.
10.6 Utilize and respond effectively to electronic and print news media.	21.9 Understand how to initiate news coverage and respond to reporters' questions.	4.12 Effective media relations are developed and maintained.
	21.10 Understand the special public relations needs that arise during crisis situations.	4.13 A comprehensive program of community relations is established.
		4.15 Community collaboration is modeled for staff.

11. Educational Law, Public Policy, and Political Systems	Domains 18, 19, & 20	
11.1 Apply knowledge of federal and state constitutional, statutory, and regulatory provisions and judicial decisions governing education.	18.4 Demonstrate knowledge of the dialectic of freedom in American education. 18.5 Identify and appreciate the tensions underlying value conflicts in American education. 18.9 Demonstrate knowledge of the various philosophical perspectives.	5.13 A comprehensive plan for community relations is established. 5.15 Opens the school to public scrutiny. 6.3 There is ongoing dialogue with representatives of diverse community groups. 6.6 Lines of communication are developed with decision makers outside the school community.
11.2 Apply knowledge of common law and contractual requirements and procedures in an educational setting.	18.10 Apply the knowledge of the philosophical perspectives in analyzing the values in our democracy and global society. 18.11 Know the standard criticisms of each philosophical perspective.	**Standard 6** 6.4 The school community works within the framework of policies, laws, and regulations enacted by local, state, and federal authorities. 6.5 Public policy is shaped to provide quality education for students.
11.3 Define and relate the general characteristics of internal and external political systems as they apply to school settings.	18.12 Understand that reality is socially constructed. 19.1 Demonstrate knowledge of federal constitutional provisions that apply to the public education system by identifying judicially recognized individual rights guaranteed by the First, Fourth, and Fourteenth Amendments to the U.S. Constitution.	
11.4 Describe the processes by which federal, state, district, and school-site policies are formulated, enacted, implemented, and evaluated, and develop strategies for influencing policy development.	19.2 Demonstrate knowledge of federal statutory and regulatory provisions that influence public education.	
11.5 Make decisions based on the moral and ethical implications of policy options and political strategies.	19.3 Demonstrate knowledge of state constitutional, statutory, and regulatory provisions governing a state's educational system.	
11.6 Analyze the major philosophical tenets of contemporary intellectual movements, and analyze their effect on school contexts.	19.4 Demonstrate knowledge of the standard of care applicable to civil or criminal liability for negligent or intentional acts under a selected state's common law or school code.	

11.7 Develop appropriate procedures and relationships for working with local governing boards.	19.5 Demonstrate knowledge of principles applicable to the administration of contracts, grants, and financial accounts in a school setting.
	20.1 Articulate the general characteristics of political systems and the manner in which those major characteristics apply to school systems.
	20.2 Describe the formal relationship between federal, state, local district, and school-site policies.
	20.3 Identify the theories of action in an existing or proposed policy.
	20.4 Assess the means-end relationships embedded in policies in light of available evidence and develop conditional recommendations regarding the ability of policy options to attain their stated aims.
	20.5 Describe how an existing or proposed policy interacts with other policies and how it complements or challenges the norms and routines of the school.
	20.6 Describe how actors in various arenas are (or are not) able to acquire the relative power advantage on particular policy issues.
	20.7 Assess the conditions under which prominent political strategies are more or less likely to be effective.
	20.8 Develop if-then scenarios that outline alternative political strategies that could be employed to mobilize support for or resistance to particular policy proposals.
	20.9 Profile the relationships in the local school setting, and indicate how these power relationships affect the likelihood that particular proposals can be enacted and implemented.
	20.10 Articulate how policy options affect particular dimensions of quality, equity, efficiency, and liberty.
	20.11 Assess policy options and political strategies in light of their moral and ethical implications.
	20.12 Assess the political interests and ideals of relevant constituent groups inside and outside the school setting.
	20.13 Define and defend the value premises and ethical principles that will guide and govern their behavior in political arenas.

AREA V. INTERNSHIP

12. Internship

12.1 Requires a variety of substantial in-school or district experiences over an extended period of time in diverse settings, planned cooperatively and supervised by university and school district personnel.

12.2 Establishes relationships with school leaders acting as trained mentors or clinical professors who guide individuals preparing for school leadership in appropriate in-school or district experiences.

12.3 Includes experiences in social service, private, and/or community organizations.

Section 2
The School-University Connection

The purpose of this section is to make the connection between what takes place in the field and the expertise supplied by the educational leadership faculty. With all the changes taking place in schools today, many interns become inundated with the day-to-day functioning of the school and their particular assignments within the internship. Through the visits of the university supervisors, the interns have the opportunity to interact with and gain insight from an individual who is not intimately connected to the school. In addition, the visits of the university supervisors provide the intern with a touchstone to discuss various aspects of the assignment, both from the university intern program and from the field-based requirements. Two key elements in this linking of school and community are the roles and responsibilities of the intern (chapter 3) and the Saturday seminar (chapter 4).

≋ Chapter 3
The Internship: Roles and Responsibilities

INTERNSHIP: NATURE AND VALUE

The purpose of any internship program is to provide experiences capable of bringing insight to professional educators who are either entering or currently practicing in public schools. An internship experience involves field placement, a firsthand work experience in which the student has an opportunity to learn how academic knowledge can be applied in the educational setting. The student becomes a participant-observer in the field under the direction of a field supervisor while receiving academic credit from a university supervisor. The intern is subject to the authority, rules, and regulations of the sponsoring school district. Through these experiences, prospective administrators may more clearly discern patterns in their administrative performance. The intern should be able to analyze the actions performed or observed with regard to administrative competence. Thus, participants gain valuable work-related experience that gives them a competitive advantage when applying for a position after graduation.

INTERNSHIP REQUIREMENTS

Before a student is approved for an internship, the following conditions must be met*:

1. A B average or higher in master's degree coursework

*The student's advisor must approve any deviation from these requirements.

2. Graduation or master's level certification requirements to be met at the conclusion of the internship quarter or semester

As part of the application process, the student must sign the student agreement (see appendix A).

If the application is approved, the student establishes contact with a school administrator and is accepted. A statement of acceptance must be completed by the field supervisor (see appendix A).

ACADEMIC CREDIT

For academic credit, the internship program stipulates eight minimum requirements.

Leadership Activities

Students should be involved in administrative activities on a weekly basis. The actual number of hours required is to be determined by each program; however, one example may be ten hours per week for a fifteen-week semester to equal 150 hours. These activities may include, but should not be limited to, activities known as duties. Field supervisors should provide meaningful tasks and ensure that the intern's activities reflect the entire scope of educational leadership. A daily log of leadership activities and observations keyed to the principal competencies must be kept by the intern (see appendix B).

The Reflective Journal

In addition to daily comments, this log should contain a weekly reflection of activities and observations. The purpose of the reflective journal is to take time to step back and analyze decisions and subsequent actions. To improve performance, self-assessment needs to become an integral part of the routine. Reflective leaders model the reflective process and are often observed coaching other staff members; the end result is improved schools. Educational leaders who regularly reflect on their actions recognize that change is inevitable and that chaos often accompanies change (Brown & Irby, 1997).

In writing a journal entry, describe the leadership situation. Who was involved in the situation? What happened? When did the situation occur? Where did the situation take place? Analyze why the situation occurred or why those involved made the decisions they did. Also, consider how the situation or decision related to the school goals or mission. Finally, discuss the relationships affected by the situation or decision.

Appraise the impact of the situation or decision on the school environment. Address the effectiveness of the decision and how student learning will be improved. Seek new understandings of the situation at hand.

Transform the situation or decision into self-growth. Explain how participating in or observing the situation led to growth. Discuss how leadership skills were enhanced. Assess which strategies could be replicated or should be changed. Finally, delineate how the situation could have been improved.

Policy and Governance

Interns are required to attend at least one school board work session and one school board meeting during the quarter or semester of their internship. A written reflection of the meeting should be attached to the agenda.

Comparison of Administrative Styles

Administrative interns are required to shadow an administrator in a school or school district other than the one where they are employed. This shadowing experience should be written in fifteen-minute intervals, contain a reflective observation, and be included in the intern's reflective journal.

School Improvement Project

The intern will complete a school improvement mini-project incorporating a minimum of six of the NCATE principal competencies (see chapter 2). This project must receive the approval of both the field and university supervisors (see appendix C). One formal presentation of this project is required for completion of the internship. (Public school standards, school of excellence, handbooks, or accreditation paper-work will *not* meet this requirement.)

Community Service Involvement

Each administrative intern is required to become an active participant in a social service, private, and/or community organization. Because of the teaching assignments of some interns, selective participation will be expected, as well as assistance at organization functions.

Leadership Portfolio

Information on this requirement is provided in chapter 5.

Saturday or Evening Seminars

Attendance at Saturday seminars is required of all interns. This topic is discussed in chapter 4.

EVALUATION

The student may receive a final grade of S (satisfactory) or U (unsatis-factory). To earn an S and academic credit, *all* course requirements must be fulfilled satisfactorily within the specified time. A grade of U earns no academic credit. Should the intern earn a grade of U, the intern's academic advisor, the university supervisor, and the intern will develop a remediation plan. The grades of S and U are not included in the computation of the grade-point average.

INTERN PERFORMANCE GUIDELINES

- Avoid becoming involved in ideological disputes. The intern's role is participant-observer. Be objective.
- Confidentiality of records and of internal matters *must* be maintained at all times. Any violation of confidentiality will result in the termi-nation of the internship with a grade of U.

- At the end of the second week of the internship, the intern will submit a school improvement project plan (see appendix C) to the university supervisor. The field supervisor should assist the intern in selecting the problem to be addressed.
- Any behavior deemed improper (detrimental to the school or university) will result in termination of the internship with a grade of U.
- All materials submitted, except the daily log, must be typed.
- All materials submitted become the property of the department of educational leadership.
- Professional dress is expected during the internship.

RESPONSIBILITIES OF THE DEPARTMENT OF EDUCATIONAL LEADERSHIP

The department has the responsibility to fully cooperate with school systems and agencies participating in the internship.

- Provide a university supervisor to coordinate activities.
- Provide information and a mentor preparation session for field supervisors at the beginning of each quarter or semester.
- Maintain monthly contact with the intern's field supervisor during the course of the internship to discuss the intern's progress. A contact report (see appendix D) will be completed by the faculty supervisor and made part of the student's permanent internship file.
- Maintain monthly contact with the intern through site visitations. During these visits, the university supervisor will discuss progress on the mini-project, portfolio development, and other matters pertaining to the intern's professional development.
- Assist in the development of the intern's leadership portfolio.
- Develop appropriate and timely Saturday or evening seminars.
- Determine the intern's final grade.
- Notify the intern if it becomes necessary to terminate the placement, and explain why termination was necessary.
- Discuss any termination with the field supervisor.

RESPONSIBILITIES OF SCHOOL
DISTRICTS ACCEPTING INTERNS

School districts have the following responsibilities.
- Provide the intern with meaningful tasks and ensure exposure to as many operational and instructional leadership aspects as possible.
- Provide a supervisor to direct and coordinate the student's internship and to prepare a written evaluation of the intern's performance (see appendix E).
- Offer constructive criticism to the intern when needed.
- Provide the facilities, supplies, and space necessary for the intern to adequately perform the assigned duties.
- Help the intern select a school improvement project.
- Alert the faculty supervisor to any problems relating to the intern's job performance.
- Request the university supervisor to withdraw the intern when personal conduct or educational progress is such that additional time and effort on the part of the school district would not be worthwhile.
- Suggest to the university supervisor how the internship program might be improved.

TECHNIQUES FOR INCREASING INVOLVEMENT BETWEEN
THE UNIVERSITY AND SCHOOL SYSTEMS

Many techniques can be used to increase the involvement of all who participate in the internship. The following is not a complete listing; it can be modified and added to, based upon the situation.

At the close of the quarter or semester prior to the start of the internship, those who will be participating in the internship are required to submit an application for the internship. Upon receipt and approval of the application (see appendix A), the student is sent a notice of the required introductory seminar (see Chapter 4). Included in this notification packet is a letter inviting the student's immediate supervisor and/or a designee to attend this session. Through their attendance at the seminar, the various schools and school systems contribute to the continuing evolution of the internship program.

Site visitations by the university field supervisor provide the university and the school with a continuing dialogue pertinent to internship development. These visits, as outlined previously, occur monthly. The Educational Leadership advisory council provides another school-university forum. This council, comprised of practicing school and systemwide administrators, meets twice yearly to discuss current practices, recent trends, and future directions for the department of educational leadership and the impact its programs and services have on local schools.

School-EDL involvement also occurs in the operation of state educational service agency consortium. In this forum, superintendents from local schools gather monthly to discuss common concerns and hear presentations on a variety of education-related topics. One of these sessions is devoted to a dialogue with several of the EDL faculty about ongoing practices in the department of educational leadership, as well as the solicitation of systemwide needs. An outcome of this dialogue may be development of a principals' or superintendents' assessment center. These centers are designed to examine potential and current administrators on various administrative leadership skills. A final outcome of these discussions may be the increased awareness of all participants for field-based action research.

BENEFITS FOR THE INTERN, SCHOOL SYSTEMS, AND UNIVERSITY

Benefits the intern accrues from participation in the program include an opportunity to put theory into practice. Through the internship, the individual gains insight into the everyday functioning of a school. Educational, social, and political influences of all of the school's publics are compared and contrasted from the perspective of administration. In addition, through the development of the portfolio and participation in the Saturday or evening seminars, the intern hones application and interviewing skills. Finally, the internship provides the student with a last opportunity to refine a leadership philosophy prior to accepting an entry-level administrative position.

School system benefits from having personnel involved in the internship include the opportunity to assess the leadership potential of aspiring administrators. With the inclusion of the mini-project as a requirement for the internship, school administrators have the opportunity to assign a needed school improvement project to a competent individual. In addition, the intern brings current theory and techniques to the school. Finally, in some cases, the university supervisor serves as an outside consultant to programs or to changes considered by the school administrator.

The university and its personnel remain current with real-world school problems, concerns, and exemplary practices. Through involvement with participating schools, the university is able to make programmatic changes based on needs observed through the process. The collaborative efforts of the university and schools can lead to continuing action-based research for the improvement of education at both levels.

☙ Chapter 4
Seminars

Students who are involved in an internship program must not feel alone in the field. They need the opportunity to converse with other interns who are experiencing some of the same challenges. In addition, it is important for the university's internship supervisors to present information to the interns in an atmosphere that resembles a classroom so that the interns can discuss the presented material with each other and their supervisors. Perhaps the most efficient method to achieve these goals is through the Saturday or evening seminar format. These seminars are approximately three hours in length. The design of a particular internship program, however, may permit seminars to be held at more appropriate times. These various designs may lend themselves to shorter "focus group" activities covering selected topics in a shorter time period. The actual seminar will be determined by the design and needs of individual internship programs.

The series of topics presented here are designed as Saturday morning seminars, but additional topics may be added, depending on the nature and length of the internship. A "constructivist classroom" approach can be used to determine additional seminar topics. The constructivist approach allows students an opportunity to suggest topics and learning activities appropriate to their needs and the context of their internship. Saturday seminars are especially attractive because interns will not have to leave their schools prior to the end of the day to attend and thus be unavailable to assist in some function at the school. The seminars must be scheduled in advance so interns can plan for substitute coverages, if needed, for athletic events, music activities, or other school-based functions to which they have been assigned. At the beginning of the internship, the students are provided with the topics to be discussed so they may arrive prepared to participate in a discussion.

Suggested topics for the seminars and focus groups include, but are not limited to, an introduction to the administrative internship, professionalism and ethics and professional dress, developing your vision and philosophy, public presentation: so you want to be an educational leader, and a Saturday of sharing (when the interns report to their peers on their internship projects and peer review portfolios; see chapter 5). In addition to these topics, various case studies and simulations are introduced through an in-basket format. These in-baskets are presented during the seminar (opening of school problems) and third Saturday seminar (closing of school problems). In addition, in-basket items are included, based on experiences at the three educational levels. The interns are provided feedback to their responses to the various situations during the university supervisor's visit to the field. (For in-basket simulations, see chapter 5.)

THE FIRST SEMINAR: AN INTRODUCTION
TO THE ADMINISTRATIVE INTERNSHIP

This first session is generally conducted prior to the start of the regular quarter or semester class schedule for the college or university. By meeting before classes begin, interns can gain additional time on needed administrative responsibility, which is critical to those interns whose certification program requires the documentation of specific internship hours. The intern's field-based supervisor is encouraged to attend this session to develop a more complete understanding of the program. In addition, field-based supervisors attending this initial session with their interns, have the opportunity to resolve any conflicts that may be apparent with the interns and their duties or responsibilities at the school.

The seminar begins with an introduction of the interns and their supervisors. Then the university faculty present the various components of the program, complete with the hourly requirements, acceptable and unacceptable internship projects, and the signing of various participation forms by the students and the field-based supervisors (see appendix A). The area of most concern for everyone involved tends to be the attainment of the required hours per week of administrative assignment, especially for those interns who are in the classroom and not already serving in an administrative capacity. All too often, this requirement has been relegated to three basic duties: before-school bus duty, cafeteria duty, and after-school bus duty. During the course of this opening seminar, the university supervisors need to stress that, as future administrators, the interns must become involved in the many facets of school management, including budget development and expenditure; curriculum revision; conflict resolution, meeting system, state, and federal policy guidelines; and discipline referrals. Any one of these can be expanded into the intern's school-based project for the course.

Following the discussion on the hourly expectations of the internship, the students are presented with the internship portfolio and weekly log. The notion of developing a living document that will highlight an individual's career path toward and in administration is novel for many of the students and their field-based supervisors. However, at the university level, portfolios are becoming a method of evaluating faculty with designs toward promotion and tenure, and in the public schools, portfolio evaluation is taking on more importance as a means of developing a qualitative approach to student assessment.

Time is allotted at the conclusion of the session for the university-based supervisor, the school-based supervisor, and the intern to meet and become acquainted. In addition, the university-based supervisor uses this time to schedule visits to the intern at the school. Finally, the meeting is used to lay the foundation for a successful internship experience.

THE SECOND SEMINAR: PROFESSIONALISM AND ETHICS

The second of the Saturday seminars has two parts: professionalism and ethics and completion of the first of two in-basket activities. In the first of these—professionalism and ethics—much of the interns' coursework throughout the certification process has focused on the content and process of administration. Most often, little time is devoted to professionalism and ethics.

PARENTS ENTRUST THE CARE OF
THEIR CHILDREN TO EDUCATORS.

These powerful words imply an enormous responsibility for educational leaders, who have a professional obligation and a duty to uphold this unwritten contract with school clients. Parents have the right to expect that their children are in the care of a professional who practices and maintains a standard of exemplary conduct. To this end, it is the responsibility of graduate schools of preparation and of the leadership student to internalize a code of ethical behavior. The purpose of this section is to set into motion an understanding of ethics and to ensure student exposure to examples of codes of ethical conduct.

Some Assumptions

Students who are accepted into graduate programs for leadership certification generally have undergraduate degrees or certification in an area of education and also classroom or student services–related experiences. These individuals are making a commitment to be role models in the school and community. It should be assumed that these future leaders have internalized a code of ethics that will distinguish them from others in the teaching or service-related ranks. However, too often this is not the case. Many individuals aspiring to be educational leaders are unaware of ethical codes of behavior and do not demonstrate professional behavior. It cannot be assumed that interns, as students and as teachers, had good leaders as role models. If there is truth to the saying that "teachers teach the way they were taught," then there may be some truth in the statement that "leaders lead the way they were led."

Interns must understand that how clients view the principal, the teachers, and the school in general is determined by how the leader leads. How people lead is based on the principles or values they embrace and how they model them through daily leadership practices.

Educators and Professionalism

Educators have consistently viewed themselves as professionals. They expect to be treated as professionals and ask for salaries commensurate with professional status. Educators have professional organizations, professional journals, professional codes of ethics, and various state licensing requirements. The question can then be asked: Why do educators continue to have difficulty in being recognized as professionals within the community and by other professionals? Three reasons could account for this lack of acceptance.

First, educators do not have a standard code of ethics they recognize and take an oath to uphold. This practice is common in the other professions with which educators equate their status. There are codes of ethics for educators, but for whatever reason educational organizations have been reluctant to embrace these codes, either individually or collectively.

Second, if an educator is accused of violating an ethical standard, the professional organization does not bring the individual before peers for a review and for administration of sanctions if found guilty. Rather, the professional education organization for teachers and administrators provides a defense for the educator against the charges.

Third, certifying agencies are not consistent in the practice of requiring successful completion of a state or national examination before licensing educators to practice. Each state determines what school levels or system levels require certification and what requirements are necessary. Recently, at least one state has required no specific area of preparation and no specific certificate for being an educational leader.

In the absence of these requirements and given the lack of consistency between governing bodies, it is the responsibility of the individual intern, the intern's school system, and the graduate school of education to assist in the internalizing of a code of professional ethics that is modeled in both personal and professional behaviors.

Codes of Ethics

Internship seminars provide the opportunity for future leaders to examine and discuss a variety of codes of ethics. The interns should have the opportunity to discuss teacher-specific, leadership-specific, and comprehensive codes of ethics (see appendix I). The intern supervisor should provide examples of local, state, or national organizations' codes for students to examine, or students may be given an assignment to research these areas. An additional resource for this seminar could be a professor from departments such as business, psychology, or philosophy, who often have an extensive background and expertise in the area of ethics. After examining the codes of ethics, interns should be given the opportunity through case studies and in-basket activities to make informed ethical decisions concerning their leadership roles (see chapter 5 for case studies and in-basket activities). Interns may discuss these case studies in small groups and then present their findings and position to the whole class. If the class of interns is small, selected case studies may be approached through whole-class discussions.

Professionalism and ethics may, at times, make the difference between a successful career and one that is marred by controversy with students, faculty, staff, administration, parents, and/or the community. Educational leaders have the responsibility of being proper role models in schools and in the community. Fulfilling this role requires practice and commitment to a set of high principles that defines the person as an individual, as an educator, and as a leader within the school community.

THE THIRD SEMINAR: PROFESSIONAL DRESS AND PRESENCE

Dress and presence make that first impression at the interview and are the image interviewers see you projecting in the position and to the public. That first impression you make may be the deciding factor in selecting you for a leadership assignment or awarding it to another. Remember, first impressions are lasting impressions, so dress and model the behavior for the position you want, not the one you have.

Interns are often oblivious to their dress and the dress of their colleagues. Determining by their appearance who is on the professional staff and who are the students, the parents, and the uncertified staff can be difficult in many schools. The administrator of a school is the individual who establishes the atmosphere of the learning environment. If the administrator is carefree and unkempt, the school will reflect that attitude. However, if the administrator is meticulous and well groomed, the school is likely to reflect those values.

Included in the discussion of professional dress is the entire picture the public sees. It is interesting to observe the manner in which school administrators who dress as professionals are received by the business community, as compared with administrators who are seen in public attired in blue jeans or collarless shirts. As our schools are commonly compared with business models and as school-business partnerships are stressed, school leaders must begin to take on the appearance of properly attired managers. There are, however, times when spirit days or pep rallies beckon administrators to shed their dress clothes for apparel more appropriate to the events. At these times a second set of clothes should be carefully placed in the office closet so that, following the event, the administrator can resume a professional appearance.

Interns must be informed that they are professionals who should dress accordingly. Many times this comes as a surprise, especially to the athletic coach or industrial arts teacher who is accustomed to much more casual attire. In these instances, the interns are requested to dress for their teaching positions (safety requirements are especially important for industrial arts teachers) but be prepared to don professional dress to perform any of their administrative duties. This area is noted by university supervisors when they visit interns in the field. Because information about professional image, dress, and interviewing is not often readily available, a rather detailed description of this part of the seminar follows.

Developing a Professional Image

We often hear the expression "clothes make the man," yet in our profession we tend to ignore the importance of dress for professional success. To succeed in any field, especially education, one must establish credibility quickly.

Importance of Professional Image

For some unknown reason, educators often believe that professional dress applies to only doctors, nurses, attorneys, bank tellers, and flight attendants. We fail to let professional dress help us every day in the classroom or school office. Every time we walk into a classroom or school building, we make a visual impression on students, parents, administrators, and other staff members.

Consider a middle school classroom with the teacher dressed in jeans, tennis shoes, and open-collared shirt as he works at his desk during his planning period. The office secretary informs him via the intercom that Mrs. Jones is on her way to his room to discuss her son's grades. Consider a second scene in which the only difference is that the teacher is wearing a pressed pair of khaki pants, a long-sleeved light blue shirt, a conservative dark blue tie, and well-polished loafers. Who do you think will immediately establish credibility in the first few seconds of the meeting? You can, of course, see the difference. The professionally dressed teacher immediately makes a statement of professional presence. Because of his dress, he appears believable.

In the first scene the teacher must work to establish the parent's confidence through what he says because his dress will tend not to favorably impress the parent. Professional educators, teachers, and administrators have an effect on students as well as on parents. Much of the impression they make is in their professional appearance. In their own work settings, educators need to be able to convey the message, "I am the educator, the person in charge of this classroom or school, and I am a positive role model for your child."

How to Begin

Those who aspire to educational leadership often ask, "Where and how do I begin?" Naturally, they must attend graduate school and earn the degree or state certificate. But prior to that, aspiring administrators can begin by dressing the part. Wearing the uniform of a school leader in the classroom portrays to others (teachers, parents, school leaders) that the would-be leader has high standards, is a role model, and has the attributes of leadership. School leaders should dress their part as they meet countless individuals from all walks of life. Through appropriate dress, these school leaders can immediately establish credibility. Appearance must work for educational leaders rather than against them.

The Administrator Uniform

Well-pressed slacks in navy, gray, black, or khaki are the foundation of the male administrative uniform. The belt and shoes should be brown or black and should match. In particular, a plain brown leather belt is preferable. Current style also has suspenders as acceptable; however, stay with solid colors that are coordinated with the rest of the attire. Shoes should be well cared for, either solid-colored dress loafers or wing tips. Although other varieties of shoes may be more comfortable, the overall appearance dictates these two styles. The shirt should be long-sleeved, regardless of the outdoor temperature, and either solid white or blue. Emphasis is placed on the sleeve length because, as a leader, you will be required to wear a suit or sport coat at various times during the day, and at those times the sleeve should extend approximately one-half inch past the end of the coat sleeve. The tie should have a small, detailed print and be coordinated. Keeping a coordinated sport coat or matching suit coat nearby, to be worn as the situation dictates, is important.

Depending on school activities, having available blue jeans, a T-shirt or sweat shirt, and sneakers may be necessary. However, this attire is unacceptable when the administrator is acting as the "leader" of the school.

Women have two choices: two-piece suits in solid colors such as navy or gray (a first choice) or a dark solid skirt, white or light-colored shirt or dress blouse, and a blazer in navy, black, or charcoal. When the weather becomes warmer, a wheat-colored suit or blazer will work well. A plain, low-heeled polished pump is non-trendy and helps one navigate the halls. Administrators must be able to get to places quickly, should an emergency arise. Hosiery can be natural or light tan, depending on the season.

The best method to enhance a woman administrator's image is to wear the conservative colors of navy, charcoal, and black. These are considered the power colors. Forest green, dark brown, and taupe are also acceptable in skirts and blazers. Women can also wear coat dresses or other executive types of dresses, usually in solid colors.

Women need to avoid pink clothing except under a black suit. Although many schools have uneven heating, wearing sweaters suggests the image of a secretary. Wearing flowers send the message that a woman is not in charge. Heavy jewelry, which tends to indicate a glitzy individual, should be avoided.

Elementary school administrators sometimes wear jumpers or blouses decorated with school prints, apples, or the like. Limit this type of clothing to special occasions. It can be difficult to establish a leadership sense of presence with parents or other system administrators while wearing this type of clothing. However, this type of clothing is acceptable to visit an elementary class for a special occasion.

The Job Interview

You have just received a most anticipated call concerning your career. A personnel director has contacted you about your application for an administrative position in a high-quality school system. An interview has been scheduled for the following week. The way you present yourself during this interview will determine if you have cleared the first hurdle in securing an administrative position or wasted the last opportunity you will have for such a position in that school system.

Plan to wear a conservative solid navy, gray, or black suit with conservative shoes in a coordinated color. Do not mix blue clothing with black shoes. Good grooming is a must. Plan a hair appointment immediately to avoid that noticeable fresh haircut look. You should not only be well groomed but also carry a natural appearance.

A neatly manicured appearance is important. A light-color polish that is coordinated with the apparel is the best bet for women. Jewelry for both men and women should be kept to a minimum. For men, a watch (preferably not a plastic athletic watch) and a wedding ring are sufficient. A woman can wear a watch, ring, small earrings, and one necklace, perhaps pearls or a thin gold chain. Above all, you do not want to be remembered for your jewelry.

Both men and women need to keep fragrances to a bare minimum, preferably in a clean scent. Florals tend to become sweet, thereby taking away from your presentation. You do not want your fragrance to arrive before you or overshadow your responses during the interview.

Practice in your mind how you will walk into the interviewer's office, keeping in mind the need to make a smooth entrance with an even stride. Walk into the interview in a confident fashion and stand tall. Good posture exhibits a businesslike character and an "I'm in control" attitude.

Upon entering, shake hands and establish eye contact. Introduce yourself by using your name. Use the name(s) of the person(s) interviewing you by thanking them for the opportunity to discuss the position. Following the introductions, be seated and wait for the interviewer to initiate the interview process. During the interview, sit tall and maintain an air of confidence. Remember, you are administrative material, and your dress, posture, and behavior confirm this.

Role-play ahead of time possible questions and answers. This is not the time to try to be totally spontaneous. Investigate beforehand the school system, the community, and the school. In addition, develop an internalized knowledge and belief system based on the following questions, which will most likely be asked during your interview.

1.   What is your philosophy of education?
2.   What are the three most important issues now facing education?
3.   What strengths do you have that will benefit this school or system?
4.   Discuss your weaknesses and what you are doing or plan to do to compensate for them?
5.   Why should we choose you over the other candidates?
6.   Where will you be, and what will you be doing years from now?

It is imperative to look at the person who asked the question when you begin giving your answers. During the answer, look at the other interviewers while occasionally smiling. Your answers should always be upbeat and positive. If you do not understand the question, ask the interviewer to repeat or rephrase the question. Do not attempt to bluff your way through a question if you do not know the answer.

If the interviewer asks if you can take on a project or develop an idea that you have not yet tried, be positive and suggest in a reassuring manner that you are capable and willing to work for the betterment of the school, system, and community. Remember, there has not been a major project that you have undertaken that you failed to accomplish.

The most effective method of demonstrating competence on the job, aside from your curriculum vitae, is through the development of a portfolio. If you have not developed a portfolio, now is the time to begin. The portfolio focuses the interview and ensuing discussion away from you the person and to your demonstrated work and activities. Keep your portfolio sharing short and centered on one or two particular items unless the interviewer shows interest in other components. The portfolio should highlight your career rather than take over the interview.

Make a conscious effort to be aware of your gestures before the interview. Concentrate on small, close-to-the-body gestures, which suggest refinement and culture, as opposed to large, exaggerated movements.

Keep your voice low at all times. Practice voice control ahead of time by humming. A conscious effort to take a full breath of air and lower the voice prior to speaking will result in a voice that is resonant and pleasant.

Standard American English is an absolute must during the interview. Record various discussions in which you are involved and analyze what you hear, or have someone else listen and provide you with honest feedback. Unless you do this, no one will critique your speech habits. Because speaking is a part of the personal self, polite people rarely correct colleagues or friends who make a spoken error in grammar. Borrow a basic grammar book and practice the use of correct English. One grammatical error during the interview can be deadly to an aspiring administrator. School personnel must know that you can communicate correctly and effectively with parents and the various publics. You will also be part of the administrative staff, the leadership of the school system, and you will be speaking for many.

Additional resources are available to assist with this seminar. A community search may locate a dress or fashion consultant who may be willing to give an in-class presentation on business dress. Major department stores often employ fashion consultants who provide this expertise as a function of their position. Major corporations often contract such services. Given corporations' interest in improving schools, they may offer to assist with this area.

If fashion consultants are not available, interns can read John Molloy's books, *Dress for Success* (1993) and *New Women's Dress for Success* (1996). An additional resource is training or instructional videos on professional dress and presence, such as *Impressions Count and So Do You!* (American Media, W. Des Moines, Iowa).

Summary

The aspiring educational leader must realize that skills, abilities, and academic preparation alone will not guarantee a leadership position. Superintendents and boards of education look for these skills but also for the public image a person presents. School leadership requires role models who are a cut above the rest and are willing to bring out the best in everyone.

THE FOURTH SEMINAR: SO YOU WANT TO BE AN EDUCATIONAL LEADER

Within the field of public school education, there are few opportunities for an individual to gain advancement without entering the ranks of leadership. Higher education has various entry levels for faculty, and businesses have various entry levels for their employees. However, in public education individuals gain advancement through only three means. The first is acquiring additional degrees or credits toward degrees. Through negotiated contracts or system pay schedules, teachers advance on a salary schedule as they accrue advanced work in their chosen field. A second way public school teachers can gain advancement is through their length of tenure within a particular school or system. This comes about through either a negotiated year-by-year salary increase or a salary schedule within the system or state. Envision a graph with credits and degrees along the horizontal and years of experience along the vertical. All one has to do to determine a salary is locate the years of experience on the vertical and move across the horizontal to the appropriate level of credits or degree. There is nearly no way for a school system to financially reward meritorious work, the development of new curricula, innovative teaching methods, or extra time given to assist students. Teachers may be paid additional money for duties such as athletic coaching, musical direction, team leadership, or club sponsors; however, these additional funds, in the form of salary stipends, are seldom calculated into the base salary of the individual. Therefore, when teachers cease to sponsor a stipend-producing activity, their salary reverts to their base of years of service and credit or degree earned.

The third method available to teachers to advance in education is to move from the classroom to the administrative office. Many beginning graduate students, when asked about their motivation for entering an educational leadership program, indicate that their primary reason for making the change from teacher to leader was finances. Although the increase in salary is definitely a plus for the move from teacher to leader, it should not be the driving force. The purpose of this seminar is to bring to the intern the realities of school leadership and insight from those who are or who have been school leaders.

Throughout their internships, these individuals will be involved in their teaching assignments and will not have an adequate opportunity to see the inner workings of educational leadership. As the seminar is designed, former and current leaders from elementary, middle, and high school are brought together to give the interns a view from the inside of the day-to-day operations in a school. This provides a supplement to the shadowing experience that is required in every internship (see chapter 3).

In discussing the role of the educational leader, it is important to stress the hours that are demanded by the job. Although leaders are not held accountable for the hours they are at school, they are expected to be the first one there in the morning and the last one to leave in the afternoon. This, of course, does not include days when there are school board meetings, parent meetings, or other school-related functions the school leader is expected to attend at night.

Another area that needs to be examined carefully is the misconception that when school is out for the summer (or vacation), nothing is taking place. When the school is closed, much of the work takes place that permits the school to run smoothly, such as developing the master schedule, ordering supplies and textbooks, and interviewing substitute and replacement teachers, to name only a few.

Perhaps the most difficult task the leader will have to handle involves evaluation of faculty and staff. Many interns profess a desire to move into a leadership role within the school or system in which they are currently teaching. Although this is a noble thought, it may be one of the most stressful assignments an administrator could ever attempt. As a teacher, the intern is one of a group of professionals working together to instruct students in various content areas, but the teacher who crosses into a leadership role is now in a position to evaluate, reprimand, and in some instances terminate a former fellow teacher.

Friendships that had seemed inseparable now are viewed in a different light. The new school leader will become privy to information that is not available to former colleagues and may become involved in matters relating to the effectiveness of faculty members or the personal lives of students. These items should not be shared with even the closest of friends because, in the event that the information is leaked, lives and careers may be permanently damaged.

It is advisable to have several other topics for this particular seminar. Because the seminar is designed to examine administrative assignments—elementary school, middle school, high school, and/or central office—it is important to bring topics to this seminar that cross division lines. Examples of such topics are the impact of special education law, state curriculum guidelines, and state law as it applies to instruction. These topics are rather precise, and an outside resource person may prove helpful.

The culminating activity to this seminar groups the students according to their areas of expertise—that is, elementary, middle, or high school. In light of their experience and the information they have gained thus far during their internships, they are asked to list three concerns for their division and to develop goals and objectives to confront and resolve these concerns. They are given seminar time to arrive at these solutions and then are required to select one individual to present the division's report to the class as a whole. Time is provided for feedback from both the professors and interns from other divisions.

As the students prepare to leave this third seminar, they are handed a packet containing their second and final in-basket. This in-basket contains situations that arise toward the end of an academic year. The students are informed that their in-basket responses will be discussed during the final visit from their university supervisor.

THE FIFTH SEMINAR: PERSONAL VISION, PHILOSOPHY, AND SCHOOL MISSION

It cannot be assumed that future leaders have a sound vision and philosophy about their purpose and place in leading a school or an educational organization. The current condition of educational practices, coupled with local, state, and national expectations, requires educational leaders to be focused and goal oriented. This cannot occur without a personal vision and an internalized philosophy of educational leadership. The internship should provide interns with the opportunity to revise, refine, and confirm those values they believe they should possess as leaders.

Interns should be provided with the opportunity to address their personal visions and philosophies during seminar activities. One activity that may be used to accomplish this is to have interns develop vision, mission, and belief statements for the hypothetical Hill Top School. This activity may be accomplished during one seminar, or various components may be incorporated into each seminar.

At the beginning of the activity, an intern is appointed principal of Hill Top School, with the other interns as faculty members. They are given the task of developing vision, mission, and "we believe" statements for Hill Top School. If the activity is completed during one seminar session, different interns should be appointed principal during various phases of the activity. If the activity is completed over several seminar sessions, a different intern should be appointed each session. Review and refinement of the document should continue until consensus is reached between principal and faculty on the document. The document prepared by the group will then become a guide for each individual intern to personalize, reflecting a specific school level as well as leadership style. An example is provide here.

Conducting this activity will introduce interns to the complicated process of working with other professionals who have varying philosophies and the difficulties experienced in reaching consensus. The intern supervisor should reinforce the need for the leader to recognize the ideas, expertise, and knowledge possessed by faculty members throughout the process. This process demonstrates the role a leader plays in developing a democratic and collaborative school culture with the faculty. It must be impressed upon interns that their level of success as educational leaders will be measured by the level of involvement, support, and followership of those they lead.

HILL TOP SCHOOL

Our vision: To be the leader in the field of education.

Our mission: To provide our students with the knowledge and skills to ensure their success in an ever changing world.

We Believe: Children first. The child's education is our first priority. The teacher will know each student's learning needs and direct him or her through developmentally appropriate activities to fulfilling these needs. The commitment from a teacher to a student mandates that all Hill Top professionals and support personnel will work to help fulfill this promise.

Respect for the individual. We provide our staff full opportunity to contribute to the success of the school through individual and group participation. We believe our teachers are professional, loyal, and supportive of the success of the school. We encourage individual initiative, inventiveness, and risk taking. The dignity of both the child and the adult is central to the way we conduct our business.

Pursuit of excellence. Our vision is to be the leader in our field. This calls for extraordinary effort by each employee. We will pursue excellence in putting educational theory into practice. Discussion of the issues is encouraged, but once a decision is made, commitment is expected from everyone. Our integrity, both as a school and as individuals, will always be without question.

Positive response to change. As society changes, so must our theories and practices of education. School employees must be future oriented and inspired by change. We are committed to help mold change to the advantage of our students and Hill Top School. Our faculty and staff will be aggressive, innovative, and positive about all internal and external affairs.

Community mindedness. The success of our educational system is directly influenced by the quality of life and the abundance of opportunities in our communities. We will work as individuals, as groups, and as a school to improve the community where we work and live.

SIXTH SEMINAR: PROJECT PRESENTATION, PEER PORTFOLIO REVIEW, AND INTERNSHIP EVALUATION

The sixth and final seminar is based around the interns and their work during the quarter or semester. This session is designed for the presentation and sharing of the interns' mini-projects, an overview of their internship experience, and a peer review of their portfolios. Each intern is required to make a ten- to fifteen-minute presentation of internship experiences, complete with keyed handouts. Within this presentation, the intern must discuss the various functions and duties performed, analyze the mini-project conducted, reflect on the school board meetings attended, and compare the leadership styles of the field-based supervisor and the person shadowed. After each presentation, fellow interns and university professors are encouraged to interact with the intern about the material presented.

Following the conclusion of the presentations, the students are given a peer evaluation form to be used as they review each other's portfolios. Each intern is required to review two portfolios and submit their completed evaluation forms to the instructors. This process allows the interns to see another individual's portfolio. Because the portfolio developed during the internship is a living document, students who see something unique in a peer's work can look for ways to include such information in their ongoing portfolio development.

At the conclusion of this seminar, the students are provided an opportunity to evaluate their internship experience through a university-designed instrument. The instrument contains a Likert scale assessment and several areas for student qualitative responses. It is through these assessment procedures that the internship program continually evolves.

OTHER POSSIBLE SEMINAR TOPICS

- The impact of special education law
- State curriculum guidelines
- Targeted selection

- Conflict resolution
- Stress management
- Teacher, parent, and community relations
- Multicultural considerations
- Technology for the administrator
- School-to-work initiatives
- School improvement plans
- Teacher empowerment
- Collective bargaining: the leadership perspective
- Site-based management
- Strategic planning

These topics, plus others students may suggest, are rather technical and may be beyond the content knowledge of the internship professor. This is an excellent opportunity to expose the interns to other professors and resource specialists from the field.

Section 3
Performance Assessment

The purpose of this section is to provide information on techniques for evaluating the leadership skills of the intern. A brief discussion of in-baskets and case studies is presented. A current trend in education is portfolio development. This section has information on how to develop the portfolio narrative and the types of support evidence that should be considered for inclusion.

⚒ Chapter 5
Skills Assessment

IN-BASKETS

The use of in-basket simulations (see appendix G) within the Saturday seminar format helps the prospective leader gain an insight into the thought process associated with educational leadership. It also assists the intern in developing a sense of connectedness between classroom work and actual practice. The constraint of time has been added to the in-basket simulation to give the intern an understanding of the limited time associated with many educational decisions. Although there are no right or wrong answers to the simulations, each has been derived from actual events. The in-baskets should not be viewed by the intern before the start of the exercise. In addition, the intern, upon completion of each in-basket, should write a reflection of the procedure used in responding to the in-basket. This exercise will provide the supervisors with insight into the intern's thought processes as he or she went about the activity.

A recommended procedure for the use of the in-baskets is to have interns complete the "Beginning of School" in-basket during the first week of the internship. By doing this, interns and their supervisors (university and field) develop a baseline about how the intern reacts under pressure. At approximately the halfway point in the internship experience, interns should respond to the set of in-baskets based upon the level (elementary, middle, or high school) at which they are currently working or the level to which they aspire. If time permits and depending upon the administrative certification in the state, interns may be required to respond to each of the in-basket sets. Finally, during the last week of the internship experience, the intern should respond to the "End of School" in-basket. Through follow-up, supervisors should be able to observe growth patterns as interns mature in their administrative internship.

Assessment of in-baskets brings about a variety of concerns. The supervisors need to have a background of experience themselves to have meaningful follow-up conversations after the completion of each set of in-baskets. Through this process, supervisors can question interns about the decision-making process and provide the intern with insights *(not answers)* to the problems presented through the in-baskets.

CASE STUDIES

The view an individual takes on an issue is influenced by that person's position relative to the issue. Teachers are likely to view educational concerns from a different perspective than leadership. The internship places interns in close proximity to leaders and their decisions, which provides interns with an opportunity to reflect upon what action was taken and what they may have done differently. Often the internship does not provide ample opportunities for firsthand critical decision making; therefore, it is necessary to provide additional opportunities.

The case study approach is an effective tool in practicing decision-making skills. Case studies in leadership provide interns with real and potential situations they may encounter as school leaders. This is an opportunity for reflective practice.Theory and knowledge can be enacted without the consequences.

The case studies in appendix H were taken from actual school events. Questions are provided to give a variety of perspectives on the issue. A response should be developed for each question that can be defended by the intern. Additional questions may be developed for each case.

THE LEADERSHIP PORTFOLIO

The recent movement toward portfolio assessment has affected both students and teachers. Now, in this time of accountability, the movement is extending to include educational leaders. According to Edgerton, Hutchings, and Quinlan (1991), portfolios are a step toward a public, professional view of education.

This section guides both the intern and the university supervisor through the steps of portfolio preparation. Field supervisors interested in preparing a portfolio, for self-evaluation or as part of a district evaluation plan, should also find the information beneficial, as should school districts moving toward portfolio assessment for their administrators.

What Is the Leadership Portfolio?

The leadership portfolio is a portrait depicting the strengths and weaknesses of the individual preparing it. Included are documents and materials that collectively suggest the scope and quality of the educational leader's administrative style. It enables administrators to display their leadership accomplishments for others to examine.

Portfolios take the assessment process past a hierarchical, often standardized evaluation system because evidence is provided from a variety of sources. The portfolio is not an exhaustive compilation of all documents related to administration. Rather, it includes selected information from coursework, leadership activities, and internship experiences. The intended outcome is solid evidence of effectiveness (Seldin, 1993).

Why Prepare a Leadership Portfolio?

There are five basic reasons for the preparation of the leadership portfolio. First, it is a mechanism for providing hard evidence of completion of the twelve guidelines outlined in chapter 2. It enables the university supervisor to assess an intern's strengths, weaknesses, and progress toward professional knowledge. Second, it is a useful tool for presenting evidence of leadership experiences in a practical and efficient manner during an interview. The ability to provide evidence to a prospective employer is indispensable. Third, interns have reported that a portfolio contributes to their professional self-confidence. The portfolio serves as a set of "tools" that administrative interns can carry with them as they progress in their careers. Fourth, it enables the educational leadership department to analyze the effects of the leadership program on the development of interns in relation to the goals and objectives of the educational leadership program. The faculty gains a deeper understanding of the strengths and weaknesses of the program. Identified program weaknesses can be targeted for improvement. Fifth, and perhaps most important, the portfolio allows interns to reflect on their beliefs, convictions, and accomplishments for the purposes of self-improvement. The process of portfolio development should cause interns to deeply consider their leadership philosophy and their beliefs about teaching and learning. These reflections should lead to improvement in performance.

What Goes in a Leadership Portfolio?

There are two parts to a leadership portfolio. First is the narrative, which is a reflective document detailing such areas as the intern's leadership and teaching and learning philosophy, leadership responsibilities, accomplishments, and improvement activities. Usually the narrative is eight to ten pages in length. Described within the narrative is what and why the intern leads others as he or she does. The leadership narrative must reflect consistency between beliefs about leadership and the intern's actions in school. Sample narratives are provided in appendix I.

The second part of the leadership portfolio is the appendix. All claims made in the narrative must be supported by evidence in the appendix. Major attention must focus on evidence supporting effective leadership.

Is Collaboration Important in Developing the Portfolio?

The portfolio process requires individual guidance by a person familiar with the process. The credibility of the portfolio is increased through the supervisory support system. The university supervisor should guide the writing process and selection of supportive evidence. Together the intern and the professor critically analyze the leadership philosophy and career objectives of the intern. They decide what types of information remain to be collected and how best to present the information developed and obtained. The university supervisor must help interns understand that portfolio development is not the collection of a "bunch of stuff" from their desks and filing cabinets but a way to analyze leadership performance for self-improvement in an effort to obtain career objectives. Portfolio development should be seen as a learning experience for both the intern and the university supervisor.

How Does One Begin the Portfolio Narrative?

It is recommended that interns begin the process of developing the narrative by answering the reflective questions listed in appendix I. These questions provide the groundwork for deciding what to include in the actual narrative. Once the questions are completed, the university supervisor reviews each response for content and to provide the intern with direction on how to proceed with writing the narrative. The university supervisor gains a deeper understanding of what the intern believes and why he or she leads in a certain manner. Often students want to skip laying the groundwork as they find some questions difficult to answer; however, without answers to these questions, writing the narrative is extremely difficult.

What Headings Might Be Used in the Narrative?

Each portfolio yields a unique portrait of the individual compiling it. The list here provides suggested narrative headings. Each intern should feel free to use any of these or none of these. Other headings developed by the intern and the university supervisor may better suit the intern's purposes. Some students even choose to include a biographical sketch in their narrative.

Leadership Philosophy
Teaching and Learning
    Philosophy
Future Leadership
    Goals/Directions
Description of Leadership
    Practices
Reflections

Improvement Activities
Awards and Recognition
Leadership Responsibilities
Assessment of Effectiveness
Analysis of Leadership
    Techniques and Strategies

Which Items Should Be Selected for Inclusion in the Portfolio Appendix?

First, it is extremely important to select items that provide evidence for the portfolio narrative. The items chosen should be applicable to both the leadership and teaching responsibilities of the intern and could include outstanding lessons developed, student work, grants written, agendas prepared, memos written, revised policies, forms created, and conference presentations. These items must be direct products of the intern.

Next, interns should include coursework from their leadership preparation program. Prior to portfolio implementation, the educational leadership department should meet to determine which assignments are to be included in the portfolio. It is preferable to select key assignments that reflect broad areas of student knowledge that are included in the leadership areas discussed in chapter 2. Students should be informed, prior to completion of the assignment, that it is to be included in their leadership portfolio. Also to be included here would be activities completed during the internship.

Finally, information obtained from others should be included, such as evaluation information that reflects areas of strength and suggestions for improvement. Supportive statements from colleagues who are knowledgeable about an intern's educational contributions can go into the portfolio, as can notes from students and the intern's honors and awards.

What Sections Should Be Included in the Appendixes?

Much like the narrative headings, appendix sections vary from portfolio to portfolio; however, there are a few sections that should be considered standard. Required sections may correspond with the programmatic model. Coursework selected to be included in the portfolio should appear in the guideline it best represents. Recommended sections include:

Professional and ethical leadership
Information management and evaluation
Instructional leadership

Professional development and human resources
Student personnel services
Organizational management
Interpersonal relationships
Financial management and resource allocation
Technology and information systems
Community and media relations
Educational law, public policy, and political systems
Examples of exemplary teaching
Workshop and conference information
Scholarly products (if applicable)
Funded grants
Information from others (leadership and teaching)
Resume or curriculum vitae

How Should I Present My Portfolio in a Large Group Setting?

In presenting the portfolio in a group setting, one should address three basic areas. First, explain what was involved in developing your leadership portfolio. Explain the processes and procedures not only for portfolio development but also for updating the portfolio. Second, display the two or three items that you are most proud of to the group. These items should be shown and discussed as each reflects your strengths as a leader. Third, explain how you have grown from the portfolio process. Within this discussion, describe your beliefs related to portfolio development for students, teachers, and educational leaders.

How Might the Leadership Portfolio Be Evaluated?

It is recommended that each portfolio be reviewed by a panel of the supervising professor and one or two other department members. Consideration should be given to including a student on the panel. Using a panel allows the analysis to be based on inter-rater reliability. An interesting concept is to have each intern evaluate the portfolios of two other interns during the last seminar. This not only gives interns experience at portfolio evaluation but also allows them to gain ideas on other types of information that they may wish to include in their own portfolios. The table in this chapter provides a rubric as a means for evaluating portfolios. In addition, within appendix I is a form with possible criteria to use in the overall evaluation of the leadership portfolio.

How Often Should the Portfolio Be Updated?

The portfolio should be considered a living document; therefore, it should be updated at least annually. Updating is based on individual preference and necessity. Interns are encouraged to keep an evidence folder in their desks. Each time they complete a task that is representative of their narrative or have something come across their desks that is worthy of inclusion in their portfolios, it should be placed in the folder. Time should be set aside on the educational leader's personal calendar to update the portfolio.

Should the Entire Portfolio Be Taken on a Job Interview?

The portfolio compiled for the internship should be considered a "master" from which to pull. Information to take on a job interview should be selected with care after a thorough examination of the job description. The information selected, along with the leader narrative and resume, should be placed in a leather portfolio. This presentation will enhance the intern's professional image.

SUMMARY

It is important for the intern, field supervisor, and university supervisor to evaluate the total internship experience both individually and collaboratively. This evaluation includes reviewing field experiences, seminar participation, and assessment materials. The intended end result is an educational leader who possess both the knowledge base and skills to be an effective leader.

Rubric for the Educational Leader's Portfolio

	Leadership Philosophy	Philosophy of Teaching and Learning	Mission and Vision	Communication Skills	Interpersonal Skills	Knowledge of Self
Unacceptable	Minimally developed leadership philosophy with coursework as supporting evidence	Minimally developed philosophy of teaching and learning with coursework as documentation	Independently developed mission or vision statement	Communicates verbally and in writing with minimal errors; appearance of portfolio is unprofessional; evidence: memos and letters to staff and parents, coursework	Facilitates groups toward accomplishment of goals; evidence: memos, letters, coursework	Self-evaluates; evidence: list of ways feedback is gathered, coursework
Needs Improvement	Leadership philosophy supported with minimal documentation: memos, letters, vision statement, mission, coursework	Teaching and learning philosophy supported with minimal evidence: memos, letters, course work	Independently developed mission and vision statement	Effective verbal and written communication with no errors; presentation of portfolio appears unprofessional; evidence: memos, letters, newsletters, coursework	Facilitates groups toward accomplishment of goals; encourages input; evidence: memos, letters from self and others, coursework	Self assesses; articulation of strengths and weaknesses of self to others; evidence: list ways feedback is collected, examples of feedback, limited discussion of self improvement plan in portfolio narrative, coursework
Acceptable	Leadership philosophy with an emphasis on instructional leadership, constructive change that leads to student improvement, and teacher empowerment with the appropriate supporting evidence: memos, letters, agendas, vision statement, mission, coursework	Philosophy of teaching and learning with supporting evidence: pictures, lesson plans, audio/videotape, coursework	Vision and mission developed with input from staff, parents, and students; evidence: agendas, memos, letters, coursework	Effective verbal, nonverbal, and written communication with students, and parents; no errors to staff, students, and parents; leadership portfolio is professional (well organized, typed dividers, etc.); evidence: memos, letters, newsletters, news releases, coursework	Facilitates groups toward accomplishment of goals; encourages input; provides support for teachers and parents; coaches staff members; evidence: memos, letters from self and others, copies of thank you notes sent, coursework	Self-assesses; articulation of strengths with minimization of weaknesses; improves weaknesses; evidence: list ways feedback is collected, examples of feedback, discussion of self-improvement plan in portfolio narrative, workshop agendas, coursework

Exceptional					
Well-developed leadership philosophy with an emphasis on instructional leadership, constructive change leading to student improvement, and teacher empowerment; encourages self and others to become risk takers in school improvement efforts; evidence: abundance of materials to include memos, letters, agendas	Well-developed philosophy of teaching and learning demonstrating an understanding of the differences between teaching children and adults, with an abundance of supporting evidence: audio/videotape of lessons taught both to students and to adults, objectives, goals, pictures	Shared vision that involves staff, parents, students, and the community in the identification and accomplishment of the school mission; evidence: agendas, minutes from meetings, memos, letters, pictures, coursework	Evidence of effective communication with faculty, staff, parents, and community; makes public professional presentations; makes time to dialogue with faculty, presents self as a professional; leadership portfolio is professionally presented; evidence: memos, letters, video	Facilitates groups toward accomplishment of goals; encourages input; provides support for teachers, parents, and community; coaches staff and other educational leaders; motivates self and others; acknowledgment of needs of all staff and students; evidence: memos, letters from self and others; copy of morale needs assessment	Self-assesses; articulation of strengths with minimization of weaknesses; improves weaknesses; seeks continuous learning activities; evidence: list of techniques for continuous feedback, examples of feedback, detailed discussion of self-improvement plan in portfolio narrative including future plans for expansion of leadership knowledge base, workshop agendas, notes of inquiry following workshop attendance, certificates, coursework

Appendix A
Internship Admission and Acceptance Forms

Application for internship

Student agreement

Immediate supervisor statement
of acceptance

DEPARTMENT OF EDUCATIONAL LEADERSHIP
INTERNSHIP IN EDUCATIONAL LEADERSHIP
Application for Internship

Name: _____ Date: _____

Social Security Number: _____ Student ID Number: _____

Home Address: _____

    City: _____ State: _____ Phone: _____

School Name: _____

School Address: _____

    City: _____ State: _____ Phone: _____

Position: _____ Years in Current Position: _____

Total Years Teaching Experience: _____

Available time for visitations: _____

Career Goal: _____

Quarter/Semester of Expected Graduation:
    ☐ Fall   ☐ Winter   ☐ Spring   ☐ Summer

List grade or indicate current enrollment in core courses.

_____

List required leadership courses completed and those of current enrollment:

COURSE	GRADE	COURSE	GRADE

Master's GPA: _____

Advisor's Approval Signature (for enrollment in the Internship):

_____

Department of Educational Leadership *Student Agreement*

I understand that I am participating in an internship sponsored by the Department of Educational Leadership and a school district. I recognize that in the internship I am subject to the rules, regulations, and policies of (Name of University), as well as those that the field supervisor deems appropriate for the school system.

I understand that I am not covered by (Name of University) fringe benefits and that it is my responsibility to make arrangements for my own insurance, including accident, health, and hospitalization coverage. I will not hold (Name of University) liable for injury or death as a result of this internship.

I understand that in the internship I will be representing both (Name of University) and the Department of Educational Leadership; I will do nothing that would adversely affect the image of either unit. I agree that if any of my behavior is deemed improper or detrimental to the school system or (Name of University), I will withdraw from the internship and accept a grade of Unsatisfactory (U).

I understand that failure to abide by the policies and procedures of the internship program will result in termination of the internship with a grade of U.

I further agree that I will:

1. Avoid becoming involved in ideological disputes.
2. Maintain the confidentiality of records and internal matters at all times.
3. Not be in possession of or use any item considered a controlled substance (except under the direction of a physician), alcohol, or firearm, while on school or university property, during my internship.
4. Always dress professionally for the internship.

I HAVE READ THIS AGREEMENT. THE NATURE, SCOPE, AND POLICIES OF THE INTERNSHIP PROGRAM HAVE BEEN EXPLAINED TO ME, AND I AGREE TO ABIDE BY THEM.

Student _____

University Supervisor _____

Date _____

IMMEDIATE SUPERVISOR
STATEMENT OF ACCEPTANCE FOR
INTERNSHIP IN EDUCATIONAL LEADERSHIP

I hereby _____ approve for an internship during Fall Winter Spring Summer Quarter/Semester 20 , and agree to assist with his/her field experiences. I understand that the internship involves a variety of administrative and supervisory experiences on-site in a school or central office setting.

I am willing to work with this intern and the (Name of University) supervising professor from the Department of Educational Leadership in developing an appropriate set of experiences and a school improvement project.

Signature of Immediate Supervisor _____

Field Supevisor Information

Name of Field Supervisor: _____

Name of School: _____ District: _____

Degree Held: _____ Certification: _____

Current Position: _____ Years of Experience: _____

Type of Teacher and/or Leadership Evaluation Preparation:

_____

Mentor Preparation: Yes _____ No _____

Appendix B
Weekly Log of Internship Experiences

NPBEA Model
Educational Leadership
Internship Experiences Checklist

Student Name: _____

Week: _____

Day of Week	Time	I. Functional Domains							II. Programmatic Domains						III. Interpersonal Domains				IV. Contextual Domains		
		1	2	3	4	5	6	7	8	9	10	11	12	13	14	15	16	17	18	19	20	21
Monday																						
Tuesday																						
Wednesday																						
Thursday																						

Friday _____

R = Responsible
P = Participated
O = Observed

Total Hours for Week _____
Total Hours Completed to Date _____

Guidelines: See chapter 2 for additional information.

AREA I: Functional domains
1. Leadership
2. Information collection
3. Problem analysis
4. Judgment
5. Organizational oversight
6. Implementation
7. Delegation

AREA II: Programmatic domains
8. Instruction and learning environment
9. Curriculum design
10. Student guidance and development
11. Staff Development
12. Measurement and evaluation
13. Resource Allocation

AREA III: Interpersonal domains
14. Motivating others
15. Interpersonal sensitivity
16. Oral and nonverbal expression
17. Written expression

Area IV: Contextual domains
18. Philosophical and cultural values
19. Legal and regulatory applications
20. Policy and political influences
21. Public relations

Student Name: _____   Week: _____

NCATE Model
Educational Leadership
Internship Experiences Checklist

Day of Week	Time	I. Strategic Leadership		II. Instructional Leadership			III. Organizational Leadership				IV. Political and Community Leadership	
		1	2	3	4	5	6	7	8	9	10	11
Monday												
Tuesday												
Wednesday												

Thursday												
Friday												

R = Responsible
P = Participated
O = Observed

Total Hours for Week ___
Total Hours Completed to Date ___
Guidelines: See chapter 2 for additional information.

AREA I: Strategic Leadership
1. Professional and ethical leadership
2. Information management and evaluation
3. Curriculum, instruction, supervision, and the learning environment

AREA II: Instructional Leadership
4. Professional development
5. Student professional services

AREA III: Organizational Leadership
6. Organizational management
7. Interpersonal relationships
8. Financial management and resource allocation

Area IV: Political and Community Leadership
9. Technology and Information systems
10. Public relations
11. Educational law, public policy, and political studies

ISLLC Model
Educational Leadership
Internship Experiences Checklist

Student Name: _____

Week: _____

Day of Week	Time	Standard 1	Standard 2	Standard 3	Standard 4	Standard 4	Standard 4
Monday							
Tuesday							
Wednesday							
Thursday							

Friday								

R = Responsible
P = Participated
0 = Observed

Total Hours for Week _____
Total Hours Completed to Date _____

Guidelines: See chapter 2 for additional information.

Standard 1: A school administrator is an educational leader who promotes the success of all students by facilitating the development, articulation, implementation, and stewardship of a vision of learning that is shared and supported by the school community.

Standard 2: A school administrator is an educational leader who promotes the success of all students by advocating, nurturing, and sustaining a school culture and instructional program conducive to student learning and staff professional growth.

Standard 3: A school administrator is an educational leader who promotes the success of all students by ensuring management of the organization, operations, and resources for a safe, efficient, and effective learning environment.

Standard 4: A school administrator is an educational leader who promotes the success of students by collaborating with families and community members, responding to diverse community interests and needs, and mobilizing community resources.

Standard 5: A school administrator is an educational leader who promotes the success of all students by acting with integrity, fairness, and an ethical manner.

Standard 6: A school administrator is an educational leader who promotes the success of all students by understanding, responding to, and influencing the larger political, social, economic, legal, and cultural context.

Appendix C
School Improvement Project Plan

School Improvement Project Plan

Name: _____ Quarter/Semester: _____

School or system: _____

Position: _____

Specific area of focus of project: _____

Objective(s):

Activities/procedures to be used:

Evaluation system:

Appendix D
Contact Report Form

Department of Educational Leadership
Internship in Educational Leadership

Contact Log

Intern: _____

Date of contact: _____ Person(s) contacted: _____

Location: _____

Comments: _____

University supervisor: _____

Appendix E
Performance Evaluation

Department of Educational Leadership
Internship
Evaluation of Student Intern

Student: _____ Quarter/Semester: _____

Field Supervisor: _____

School: _____

Please use the chart below in evaluating the performance of the student who has interned in your school. When completed, this evaluation form should be returned to the university supervisor, by the field supervisor.

	Superior	Above Average	Average	Below Average	Unsatis-factory	Unable to Observe
Punctuality/attendance						
Ability to delegate						
Appropriate attire						
Community involvement						
Ability to organize and perform tasks						
Information seeking ability						
Problem analysis						
Decisiveness						
Ability to use supervision (seek and use help, accept criticism)						
Personal motivation						
Judgment						
Commitment to legal, ethical, and moral responsiveness						
Written communication						
Oral communication						
Sensitivity						
Interpersonal relations						
Ability to work with support staff						
Ability to cope with stress						
Ability to communicate with faculty						
Ability to relate to students						
Sensitivity to diversity issues						
Range of interests						
Overall leadership performance						

Comment on the intern's strengths.

_____

_____

_____

_____

What areas would you recommend the intern to concentrate on in his or her continued professional development?

_____

_____

_____

_____

Please comment on any other aspects of the student's internship performance.

_____

_____

_____

_____

Brief description of intern assignments:

_____

_____

Note: This evaluation will be kept confidential.

_____   _____
Signature of Field Supervisor   University Intern Supervisor

_____   _____
Date   Date

Appendix F
The AASA Code of Ethics

Overview

High standards of ethical behavior for the professional school administrator are essential and are compatible with his faith in the power of public education and his commitment to leadership in the preservation and strengthening of the public schools.

Policy 1

The professional school administrator constantly upholds the honor and dignity of his profession in all his actions and relations with pupils, colleagues, school board members, and the public.

Policy 2

The professional school administrator obeys local, state, and national laws, holds himself to high ethical and moral standards, and gives loyalty to his country and to the cause of democracy and liberty.

Policy 3

The professional school administrator accepts the responsibility throughout his career to master and to contribute to the growing body of specialized knowledge, concepts, and skills which characterize school administration as a profession.

Policy 4

The professional school administrator strives to provide the finest possible educational experiences and opportunities to all persons in the district.

Policy 5

The professional school administrator applying for a position or entering into contractual agreements seeks to preserve and enhance the prestige and status of his profession.

Policy 6

The professional school administrator carries out in good faith all policies duly adopted by the local board and the regulations of state authorities and renders professional service to the best of his ability.

Policy 7

The professional school administrator honors the public trust of his position above any economic or social rewards.

Policy 8

The professional school administrator does not permit considerations of private gain or personal economic interest to affect the discharge of his professional responsibilities.

Policy 9

The professional school administrator recognizes that the public schools are the public's business and seeks to keep the public fully and honestly informed about their schools.

Appendix G
In-Basket Assessments

In-Basket   Beginning of the Year

In-Basket   Elementary School

In-Basket   Middle School

In-Basket   Senior High School

In-Basket   End of the Year

Beginning of the Year

Background

You are Dr. Smith, and you are beginning the first day of your first year as principal of Hill Top School. It is Monday morning, August 16, less than one week before the students return. Your faculty, all of whom were hired by your predecessor, Mr. Wells, will be coming back over the next two days to ready their rooms for the start of school and in preparation for their three days of preplanning meetings. You are about to check your mail, memos, e-mail, and telephone messages. You have been out of town since Wednesday evening as the result of a family emergency.

Instructions

1. You will be given sixty minutes to read and take action on all of the in-basket items presented following the instructions. You are not expected merely to describe what you would do—you are to do it. For example, if you decide to write a letter, then compose the letter. If you decide to telephone an individual or have a conference with someone, then outline your objectives as well as the main points or questions that you would present.
2. Each of the in-basket items requires action, which you should present on a separate sheet of paper. Attach the action you develop to the in-basket item it addresses.
3. Proceed to the in-basket items.

Beginning-of-the-Year In-Basket Item #1

Telephone Message

WHILE YOU WERE OUT

To: Dr. Smith

From: Elsie Mayhem, Secretary

Re: Lead article, Mr. Robert Sadler, Editor, *Journal ViewPoint* Newspaper

Date: August 10

Since I knew you'd be getting in Monday morning, I scheduled your interview with my brother for Tuesday afternoon at 1 PM. I thought it would really be a good idea to have him do an article on you as you begin your first year as our educational leader.

Beginning-of-the-Year In-Basket Item #2

Dear Dr. Smith,

Let me be among the first to welcome you to Hill Top School. This school has been one of my fastest growing accounts, exceeding $23,000 in gross sales during its annual candy bar sale last year. Much of this growth can be attributed to your predecessor, who realized what extra money could do in making opportunities available to students and staff alike.

This year's promotion kickoff has been scheduled for October 19. With some of the new prizes we have obtained, I'm sure that this campaign will be the best ever. I will be dropping by in the near future to discuss our kickoff assembly and some of the really great ideas I have for promoting your school's campaign.

I look forward to our meeting.

Sincerely,

Wes Formore, Regional Rep.

Beginning-of-the-Year In-Basket Item #3

Dear Dr. Smith,

As the new school year draws close, I want to be among the first in the community to welcome you to your new challenge. As I am sure you have heard by now, although a good-hearted person, Mr. Wells left a good deal to be desired when it came to school leadership.

My wife and I tried on numerous occasions to have our Bible study group meet during the first period for any interested student, but Mr. Wells failed to see the value of such an inspirational time. Rather, he kept telling us that we could not use school property or school time to discuss the ramifications of today's problems as they relate to the Scriptures.

As a taxpayer in this community, we request your assistance in seeing that our community's children have the opportunity to relate their problems to the Lord. We are available to meet with you and discuss a starting date and time.

Sincerely,

Rev. Billy Joe Emmanuel

Beginning-of-the-Year In-Basket Item #4

Dr. Smith—

On behalf of the Hill Top School Booster Club, we want to welcome you to the first of many successful years with our school and community. Our booster club supports not only athletics within our school but also academic pursuits. At the present time we are completing the purchase of a network server for the school so each classroom will have the capability to go onto the "Information Superhighway."

The primary method we have used to fund our projects has been through our annual candy sale. Last year, we grossed $23,000, but we realized a profit of only $8,500. According to Mr. Wes Formore, the candy sale rep, the remaining money was used for promotion and prizes. We think we can do better! Our executive committee has been meeting over the summer and we have come up with ideas we need to discuss. We just think that we can do better than a 37% profit margin.

Please give me a call so we can set up a meeting to discuss our plans.

Sincerely,

Elizabeth Dwill

Beginning-of-the-Year In-Basket Item #5

To: Dr. Smith

From: Elsie

Re: Speaker for preplanning meeting

Date: 8/12, 3:15 PM

Just got a call from Jonathan Elderson. He has been rushed to the hospital with an emergency appendectomy and will not be able to keynote the preplanning workshop, scheduled by Mr. Wells, on Wednesday morning. I didn't want to disturb your last weekend at home before the "rat race" begins so I waited to tell you. Perhaps you could do one of those talks that the interview committee heard you give.

Beginning-of-the-Year In-Basket Item #6

To: All Administrators in the HT School System

From: Dr. Roberta Conrad, Superintendent

Re: Weekly administrative meetings

Date: 8/10

As we prepare for another fantastic year at HTSS, I would like all of you to circle Tuesday mornings beginning the week of 8/16 at 8:30 for our weekly administrative sessions. I am asking Dr. Smith, the new principal at the Hill Top School, to serve as our host for our first meeting so we all get an opportunity to visit in the newly refurbished school. The remaining meetings for this month will rotate as before.

I look forward to seeing all of you on August 17. Please be prepared to share your career goals for the coming year.

Beginning-of-the-Year In-Basket Item #7

Dr. Smith—

I'm sure that you have heard several stories by now about Mr. Wells and his style of leadership or lack thereof. For the past five years I have been trying to convince him that this school is getting soft on discipline—for students as well as staff. Many of the staff members leave the school during the day to "go to the bank" or "run errands." Meanwhile, those of us who remain behind are left with two classes to watch, phones to answer, or messages to take. As a teacher, I am not paid to take messages or answer the office phone; I'm paid to teach! My classes—one at a time!

From what we have all heard about you, the behavior that existed previously will not be tolerated. Let me say, "Thank goodness for that." I look forward to working closely with you so that we can bring some respect back to the teaching profession and to the reputation of Hill Top School.

Sincerely,

Joseph P. Whitehead, Chair
Science Department

Beginning-of-the-Year In-Basket Item #8

MEMO

To: All building principals

From: Hazel Forney, Transportation

Re: Change of bus routes

Date: 8/11

As I am sure you all know by now, the new bus schedule has been mailed to each student's home and has been printed once in the *Journal ViewPoint*. Pretty much, the routes are the same as last year's with one exception. The first run in the afternoon leaves the Hill Top School five minutes earlier than last year so we can be sure to have enough time to be back for the athletic practice run. This should not be any big deal since HTSS already exceeds the state minimum for education time in all of our schools by twenty-eight minutes per week.

If you have any questions, please give me a call or see me at the boss's meeting before preplanning.

Beginning-of-the-Year In-Basket Item #9

To: Dr. Smith

From: Elsie

Re: Faculty room price increase

Date: 8/11

The Pepsi man just told me that with the increase in the price of Pepsi we would have to raise the price per can in the lounge from .60 to .75. This will still leave us with a six cents per can profit for the slush fund. Since you were not available last week, I told him to go ahead and make the change on the machine. I hope you agree.

Beginning-of-the-Year In-Basket Item #10

8/12

Dr. Smith,

I'm sorry to hit you with something like this right off the bat, but our school has consistently been short-changed within the music department. There is a tremendous amount of pressure placed on me, my staff, and the students to have a winning, eye-appealing, musical band show, but Dr. Conrad and that lackey of an athletic director she has NEVER had our practice field lined. And since no one but God and the football team can ever get on the football field except for games, we need HELP!

Please see what you can do about at least getting our field lined so when we go out on a Friday night we at least look like we practiced.

Thanks, and once again, sorry for hitting you with this so soon.

Jim Taylor, Band Director
P.S. Welcome to Hill Top School

Beginning-of-the-Year In-Basket Item #11

8/12

Dr. Smith,
I know you are extremely busy; however, I am just letting you
know that all the principals get together for lunch every Wednesday
at noon at Bigelow's. There are no APs, central office types, or
secretaries—just the six of us. I'll stop by to pick you up at 11:30
Wednesday morning—the first lunch is on me.

Bill

Beginning-of-the-Year In-Basket Item #12

8/12/95

Dear Dr. Smith,

   Let me join with other members of the school community in welcoming you to the Hill Top School. As president of the Hill Top PTO, we provide a variety of educational offerings for parents and friends of the school. In addition, we combine forces with the Booster Club in sponsoring the school's annual fund-raiser.

   Our first meeting for the new school year will be held on Tuesday, August 31, at 7:30 PM in school's newly remodeled auditorium. This meeting is generally our best attended of the year. We are inviting you to be our guest speaker. This would be a great opportunity for you to present your views on the school and to meet your students' parents. I'll give you a call the week of the 16th to see if you will accept my offer.

   Best wishes for a great year.

                                                      Sincerely,

                                                      Georgiana Wellman

Elementary School

Elementary School In-Basket Item #1

To: Dr. Smith <jsmith@htschool.k12.edu>

From: Mrs. Keyesworth, 3rd grade lead teacher
        <keyeswor@htschool.k.12.edu>

Re: Team Meeting on Tuesday

Date: 10/1

The third-grade team would like you to present our outstanding student awards at the Students of the Month ceremonies this year. As you know, these awards are given each month, and having the principal of the school present them gives them added meaning to the students and their parents. If you would like to review the criteria for student selection, please let me know and I will attach them to an e-mail for you.

Looking forward to your reply.

Elementary School In-Basket Item #2

9/14

Dear Dr. Smith,

I am writing you as a concerned parent and taxpayer of this community. My fifth-grade daughter came home from school yesterday and told me that several of the boys carry knives to school. Although she says she didn't see any knives, she is scared to come to school, and I must admit that I am afraid to send her until I can be assured that she will be safe. At first I thought she was making this up because of recent events in the newspaper; however, after listening to her talking to her friends on the phone, I'm convinced that something is going on.

Will Hill Top Elementary be the next school we read about in the paper? Something has got to be done to protect our children. We parents do all we can at home, but what are you doing at the school? Why do you allow elementary school children to have knives in school?

Sincerely,

Mrs. Wanda Borken

Elementary School In-Basket Item #3

9/28

Doc—

I'm the driver of bus 15. There are about 48 elementary school and middle school kids who ride my bus every morning and afternoon. The side the elementary school kids sit on is just tore up all the time with paper and stuff on the floor, chewing gum under the seat, and dirty words written in ink on the seatbacks. My first thought is to throw the whole bunch of them hoodlums off the bus, but Ms. Forney, the transportation director, says that I got to put it in writing to you. Here it is. I ain't going to put up with this anymore.

Bobbie, Bus 15

Elementary School In-Basket Item #4

10/3

To: Dr. Smith <jsmith@htschool.k12.edu>

From: eblayloc@htschool.k12.edu

Date: 9/24

Re: Booster Club Meeting

Jim—

Thought I'd give you a heads-up. The Basketball Booster Club at my school is meeting next week, and the topic of having your elementary school start a Saturday morning basketball program for boys and girls is going to come up again. This time, though, they are having Jackie Wainwright, my varsity coach, lead the fight. His gripe since he lost his starting team because of graduation last year is that he can't afford the time to teach the underclassmen his style and the fundamentals at the same time. He has told me that the intramural program at the middle school is a "sissy's approach" to anything. He wants to get the kids at your level starting to play basketball so they can get interscholastic experience at the middle school level and then be ready for his high school varsity.

Don't know what you can do. Just thought I'd put you wise to his doings.

Elementary School In-Basket Item #5

To: Dr. Smith <<u>jsmith@htschool.k12.edu</u>>

From: <u>carrier@htschool.k12.edu</u>

Date: 9/27

Re: Problem on Bus 15

Jim—

Last night after his last run, the driver of bus 15, Bobbie McDonahan, came in to see me. He was all upset about the problems on his bus, and he was blaming your kids for it. He said they were writing on the seats, putting gum under the seats, and generally giving him a rough time. I told him that if he was sure the troublemakers were elementary school kids (I can't really see them doing this—probably the middle school kids are the ones to blame), he should let you know. However, I know you're new to the system, and I thought I'd give you a bit of background.

Bobbie thinks at times that he's one of the kids and at times has encouraged the kids to do some crazy things. Anyway, he sometimes is so easygoing with the older kids but just the opposite with the younger kids. I usually listen to him blow off, and then he goes about his job.

Anyway, I just thought I'd let you know what I heard last night. He might not even say anything after he thinks it over.

Elementary School In-Basket Item #6

10/3

Dr. Smith,

As a newcomer to the Hill Top community, I would like to request permission to conduct informational sessions on the ways of Islam for students at your school. Children in your school are at an age where they have questions about the various religious sects, and through my instruction, I could answer their questions and help them to become enlightened about the Prophet. As highly charged as the issue of religion can become, I can assure you that by meeting interested students after school once each week, I could help to diffuse potential problems between various groups which, in the long run, would help your colleagues at the middle school and high school.

Please let me know when we can meet to establish the time and place for my meetings.

Thank you for your time,

Raoul Shantar

Elementary School In-Basket Item #7

To: Dr. Smith <jsmith@htschool.k12.edu>

From: emayhem@htschool.k12.edu

Date: 10/2

Re: What I've heard

Yesterday after church, at our coffee social, Wanda Borken had a crowd of folks gathered around her. I happened by just close enough to catch the drift of what was being said and understood her to say that her daughter told her that we were allowing kids to bring knives to school. Not wanting to appear to be eavesdropping, I kept talking to my circle of friends. However, she was really gathering a group and stirring things up. Just thought you should know about this.

Elementary School In-Basket Item #8

To:	Dr. Smith <jsmith@htschool.k12.edu>
From:	jwilkins@htschool.k12.edu
Re:	4th-grade science books
Date:	9/26

Last year we ordered new textbooks for our fourth-grade science classes, knowing that the third grade had 64 more students than we had in last year's fourth grade. Well, now that the FTEs are in for this fall, we are 37 books short. We ordered enough to meet our needs, but the redistricting that we thought would be thrown out was approved, and we inherited over 30 additional fourth graders. What can we do? Our teachers have been copying materials to try to make up for the shortage of textbooks, but you know the problem with that. Is there any chance we can have some additional funds to buy some more textbooks?

Jane Wilkins, Hill Top School System Science Coordinator

Elementary School In-Basket #9

Doc—

Thought I'd give you a note to let you know that the swing set on the primary wing's playground has rusty chains holding the seats. In the past Mr. Wells got money to replace the chains from somewhere, but heaven only knows from where (he always seemed to have money stashed somewhere). Anyway, what do you want me to do about the chains? Do you want to see the swings I'm talking about? Let me know what you want and I'll do it.

Eddie, Head Custodian

Elementary School In-Basket Item #10

10/2

Dr. Smith,

My son rides bus 15 every day to and from school. He told me that yesterday afternoon the driver stopped the bus and started cussing at the elementary school students because he said they were destroying his bus. He said that the driver threatened to throw all the elementary school kids off the bus because they were "little babies" and writing on the seats and sides of the bus. Meanwhile, my son said that the middle school kids were yelling and telling him to throw the elementary school kids off. Why is this driver so mean to elementary school kids? My son said that the middle school kids can do and say anything they want, and he doesn't do anything to them. What is going on with this guy? And it's not just my son. Other parents have said that their kids have told them the same things.

Please help us get to the bottom of this. He's got our kids' lives in his hands, and the way he acts, he's been scaring the kids and me.

Sincerely,

Ken Matheson

Elementary School In-Basket Item #11

To: Dr. Smith <jsmith@htschool.k12.edu>
From: eboone@htschool.k12.edu
Re: Outstanding Student Ceremony
Date: 10/1

I assume that you have been informed about the Outstanding Student Ceremony that is held by the third-grade team each month. The teachers have always invited the parents and grandparents of the students who were being selected to attend, and last year Mr. Wells began a tradition of having light refreshments after the awards. Do you want to continue this tradition? What would you like us to prepare? Please keep me posted.

Ellen Boone, Cafeteria Coordinator

Elementary School In-Basket Item #12

To: Dr. Smith <jsmith@htschool.k12.edu>

From: emayhem@htschool.k12.edu

Re: Monthly fire/tornado drill

Date: 9/28

Now that we've got the year off and running, I need to remind you that we are required to hold either a fire drill or a tornado drill each month. Mr. Wells had me draw up a list of dates and post this in the faculty room so the teachers would not be caught off guard. Do you want me to draw up a list of dates for the faculty and post it? Which should be first, fire or tornado?

Middle School

Middle School In-Basket Item #1

To: Dr. Smith <jsmith@htschool.k12.edu>

From: Mrs. Keyesworth, Sixth-grade team leader
          <gogreen@htschool.k.12.edu>

Re: Team Meeting on Tuesday

Date: 10/1

On behalf of the Big Green Team, we would like you to present our outstanding student awards at the Students of the Month ceremonies this year. As you know, these awards are given each month, and having the principal of the school present them gives them added meaning to the students and their parents. If you would like to review the criteria for student selection, please let me know and I will attach them to an e-mail for you.

Looking forward to your reply.

Middle School In-Basket Item #2

9/14

Dear Dr. Smith,

I am writing you as a concerned parent and taxpayer of this community. My daughter came home from school yesterday and told me that several of the boys carry knives to school. Although she says she didn't see any knives, she is scared to come to school, and I must admit that I am afraid to send her until I can be assured that she will be safe. At first I thought she was making this up because of recent events in the newspaper; however, after listening to her talking to her friends on the phone, I'm convinced that something is going on.

Will Hill Top be the next middle school we read about in the paper? Something has got to be done to protect our children. We parents do all we can at home, but what are you doing at the school? Why do you allow middle school children to have knives in school?

Sincerely,

Mrs. Wanda Borken

Middle School In-Basket Item #3

9/28

Doc—

I'm the driver of bus 15. There are about 48 middle school and high school kids who ride my bus every morning and afternoon. The side the middle school kids sit on is just tore up all the time with paper and stuff on the floor, chewing gum under the seat, and dirty words written in ink on the seatbacks. My first thought is to throw the whole bunch of them hoodlums off the bus, but Mr. Carrier, the transportation director, says that I got to put it in writing to you. Here it is. I ain't going to put up with this anymore.

Bobbie, Bus 15

Middle School In-Basket Item #4

10/3

To: Dr. Smith <jsmith@htschool.k12.edu>

From: eblayloc@htschool.k12.edu

Date: 9/24

Re: Booster Club Meeting

Thought I'd give you a heads-up. The Basketball Booster Club at my school is meeting next week, and the topic of having your middle school start an interscholastic basketball team is going to come up again. This time, though, they are having Jackie Wainwright, my varsity coach, lead the fight. His gripe since he lost his starting team because of graduation last year is that he can't afford the time to teach the underclassmen his style and the fundamentals at the same time. He has told me that the middle school intramural program is a "sissy's approach" to anything.

Don't know what you can do. Just thought I'd put you wise to his doings.

Middle School In-Basket Item #5

To: Dr. Smith <jsmith@htschool.k12.edu>

From: carrier@htschool.k12.edu

Date: 9/27

Re: Problem on Bus 15

Last night after his last run, the driver of bus 15, Bobbie McDonahan, came in to see me. He was all upset about the problems on his bus, and he was blaming your kids for it. He said they were writing on the seats, putting gum under the seats, and generally giving him a rough time. I told him that if he was sure the troublemakers were middle school kids, he should let you know. However, I know you're new to the system, and I thought I'd give you a bit of background.

Bobbie thinks at times that he's one of the kids and at times has encouraged the kids to do some crazy things. Anyway, he sometimes is so easygoing with the older kids but just the opposite with the younger kids. I usually listen to him blow off, and then he goes about his job.

Anyway, I just thought I'd let you know what I heard last night. He might not even say anything after he thinks it over.

Middle School In-Basket Item #6

10/3

Dr. Smith,

As a student in the eighth grade, I would like to ask your permission for me to read several passages from the Koran every morning right after the announcements. Many of the students in the school ask me about my religion and don't seem to understand that although my beliefs are different than theirs, they still deserve respect. The comments that the students make when my mother comes to pick me up after band practice really upset me, and I think that if they could only hear the word of the Prophet they would change their minds and stop calling me and my family names.

Thank you for your time,

Raoul Shantar

Middle School In-Basket Item #7

To: Dr. Smith <jsmith@htschool.k12.edu>

From: emayhem@htschool.k12.edu

Date: 10/2

Re: What I've heard

Yesterday after church, at our coffee social, Wanda Borken had a crowd of folks gathered around her. I happened by just close enough to catch the drift of what was being said and understood her to say that her daughter told her that we were allowing kids to bring knives to school. Not wanting to appear to be eavesdropping, I kept talking to my circle of friends. However, she was really gathering a group and stirring things up. Just thought you should know about this.

Middle School In-Basket Item #8

To: Dr. Smith <jsmith@htschool.k12.edu>
From: jwilkins@htschool.k12.edu
Re: 7th-grade science books
Date: 9/26

Last year we ordered new textbooks for our 7th-grade science classes, knowing that the sixth-grade had 64 more students than we had in last year's 7th grade. Well, now that the FTEs are in for this fall, we are 37 books short. We ordered enough to meet our needs, but the redistricting that we thought would be thrown out was approved, and we inherited over 30 new 7th-graders. What can we do? Our teachers have been copying materials to try to make up for the shortage of textbooks, but you know the problem with that. Is there any chance we can have some additional funds to buy some more textbooks?

Jane Wilkins, Hill Top Science Coordinator

Middle School In-Basket Item #9

To: Dr. Smith <jsmith@htschool.k12.edu>

From: emayhem@htschool.k12.edu

Re: Test Results

Date: 10/3

The *Chronicle* education reporter called and wanted to set up an appointment with you to discuss your feelings about our students' showing on the Metropolitan Achievement Test last spring. I told her that you were just starting and would need some time to review them. She asked if you'd call her next week to set the day and time.

Middle School In-Basket Item #10

10/2

Dr. Smith,

My son rides bus 15 every day to and from school. He told me that yesterday afternoon the driver stopped the bus and started cussing at the middle school students because he said they were destroying his bus. He said that the driver threatened to throw all the middle school kids off the bus because they were "immature jerks." Meanwhile, my son said that the high school kids were yelling and egging him on to throw the middle school kids off. Why is this driver so mean to middle school kids? My son said that the high school kids can do and say anything they want and he doesn't do anything to them. What is going on with this guy? And it's not just my son, other parents have said that their kids have told them the same things.

Please help us get to the bottom of this. He's got our kids' lives in his hands, and the way he acts, he's been scaring the kids and me.

                                        Sincerely,

                                        Ken Matheson

Middle School In-Basket Item #11

To: Dr. Smith <jsmith@htschool.k12.edu>
From: eboone@htschool.k12.edu
Re: Outstanding Student Ceremony
Date: 10/1

I assume that you have been informed about the outstanding student ceremony that is held by the sixth-grade team each month. The teachers have always invited the parents and grandparents of the students who were being selected to attend, and last year Mr. Watkins began a tradition of having light refreshments after the awards. Do you want to continue this tradition? What would you like us to prepare? Please keep me posted.

Ellen Boone, Cafeteria Coordinator

Middle School In-Basket Item #12

To: Dr. Smith <jsmith@htschool.k12.edu>

From: emayhem@htschool.k12.edu

Re: Monthly fire/tornado drill

Date: 9/28

Now that we've got the year off and running, I need to remind you that we are required to hold either a fire drill or a tornado drill each month. Mr. Watkins had me draw up a list of dates and post this in the faculty room so the teachers would not be caught off guard. Do you want me to draw up a list of dates for the faculty and post it? Which should be first, fire or tornado?

High School

High School In-Basket Item #1

24 October

Dr. Smith,

I am writing to inform you of the travesty that occurred last Tuesday evening. At that time, Ms. Phillips conducted the tryouts for basketball cheerleaders and my daughter, Elizabeth, was NOT selected. Elizabeth has been a cheerleader for the past three years, and now, in her senior year, she is cut from the squad. I am sure you can imagine the turmoil that has been going on in our home ever since the results were announced.

Ms. Phillips is new to our system and has no idea how hard Elizabeth has worked to make the squad every year. The comment was made that this year's basketball cheerleaders would have to be more athletic. May I remind you that these girls are not playing the basketball game, they are cheering at the game.

What are we to do? How can we help our daughter regain her self-esteem? My husband and I want you to look into the way these tryouts were conducted before we get our lawyer involved. Please let me know what you find.

Sincerely,

Mrs. Nancy Culverson

High School In-Basket Item #2

Office of the Superintendent
Hill Top School System
Dr. Roberta Conrad, Superintendent

22 October

Dr. Smith,

I just received a phone call from Mrs. Nancy Culverson about the problems her daughter, Elizabeth, had with the cheerleading tryouts. Mrs. Culverson explained that the cheering coach is new this year and that she may have not conducted the tryouts fairly.

Please look into this matter and keep me posted as to your progress. Since Fred Culverson has been elected to the school board, he has been a very positive influence within the community. We don't need to have something as minor as cheerleading tryouts turn him against us.

Roberta

High School In-Basket Item #3

October 18

Dr. Smith,

I finally got a job so I can begin to earn some money for college. My job starts at 2 PM, after my academic classes are over, and I can work 6 hours each day. The only problem is that the secretary told me that there are no student parking spaces left. I see that there are at least four spaces in the faculty lot, and why couldn't I park there?

This job is really important to me, and if I can't get a place to park I won't be able to make it from school to my home and then to work.

Please help me get a parking space so I can keep my job.

Bobbie Alexander

High School In-Basket Item #4

To: Dr. Smith <jsmith@htschool.k12.edu>

From: egriffin <egriffin@htschool.k12.edu>

Re: Homecoming Dance preparations

Date: October 21

The Homecoming Committee has decided to rent the city field house for the homecoming dance so that more townspeople can attend to hear the Wave Factory. We need to have your okay for this venture because it means that we will not have the dance on campus. Ticket sales should be real good, which will help us pay for the rental of the field house as well as the band. When would be a good time for you to look over the contract and sign it? Please let me know ASAP.

Ellen Griffin, Homecoming Advisor

High School In-Basket Item #5

10/25

Dr. Smith—

Ever since my family moved to this area several years ago, we have noticed that there is a great emphasis on promoting religion within school. We approached your predecessor, Mr. Wells, on several occasions to ask for the establishment of an athletic organization devoted to Islamic athletes like the one that meets for Christian athletes. He never gave us a rationale why the Christian organization could exist and ours could not.

As you know, some of our best basketball players attend the local mosque and feel uncomfortable with the emphasis placed on religion by the coaching staff and the school as a whole. All we are asking is that those students who are followers of Islam be permitted the same rights as their Christian peers. We have checked with the local ACLU chapter, and they have told us that we have that right.

Please let me know of your decision so we may determine our next step.

Karem Ishtal

High School In-Basket Item #6

The Law Offices of Smith, Early, and Comer
2500 Center Ave.
Hill Top

23 October

Dear Dr. Smith,

This letter is to inform you that our firm represents the interests of Ms. Lori Ann Whitman, an eleventh-grade student in your school. According to Ms. Whitman, Mr. Allen Hackman, a science teacher in your school, made an unwarranted advance toward her following a discussion after class. At the request of Ms. Whitman's parents, we would like to meet with Mr. Hackman and you to assure that, if this action continues, the Whitmans are prepared to seek legal redress on behalf of their daughter.

Please contact our office to establish an acceptable time for our meeting to occur.

Sincerely,

J. W. Smith, Esq.

High School In-Basket Item #7

10/22

Dr. Smith—

My wife and I are just about fed up with what's going on at the Hill Top School. We have had three of our children graduate from HTS, and our youngest, Eddie, is now a sophomore. The other day, he got his third straight "F" in math from Mrs. Eastwick. When he asked her how he could have gotten an "F" since he made only a few mistakes in figuring, she told him that she didn't answer to any dumb kid's questions, and if he didn't like it, he could see the worthless principal down the hall.

All of our kids have had Mrs. Eastwick somewhere along the line, and none of them liked her. But Dr. Smith, our kids are good kids and have always treated teachers with respect. With Eddie in only 10th grade, what's to say that he won't have her next year or the year after. We can't stand to see our kid hurt by someone who doesn't seem to care. We don't know where to turn. We've asked to see Mrs. Eastwick to discuss the matter, but she says she's too busy.

Please help us so Eddie doesn't get turned off to school when he still has two more years to go.

Thank you.

Bill and Gretchen Yates

High School In-Basket Item #8

To: Dr. Smith <jsmith@htschool.k12.edu>

From: B. Masters <bmasters@htschool.k12.edu>

Re: Something is happening

Date: October 20

I think you should be aware that this morning when I stopped for my morning paper at the Jiffy Mart I overheard a group of boys with Hill Top School sweatshirts on talking about killing someone for asking someone's girlfriend on a date. I tried not to appear like I was eavesdropping, but I really wanted to know who they were and who they were after. They finished their conversation and got into what looked like a fairly new BMW and headed toward the school.

It might just be that I listen to the news too much, but with what has happened recently in other schools, I thought you may want to know about this.

Barbara Masters

High School In-Basket Item # 9

To: Dr. Smith <jsmith@htschool.k12.edu>

From: A. Hackman <ahackman@htschool.k12.edu>

Date: October 22

Re: Lori Ann Whitman

I don't know how to begin this, but I think that one of the girls in my junior chemistry class has a crush on me. She has been staying after everyone else has left and has been asking questions that were covered thoroughly in class. This all started about 4 weeks ago, and at first I thought she was having difficulty with chemistry, so I was eager to work with her, as I would with any student. But the other day, she started asking me personal questions, and I told her that questions like that were not part of chemistry class, but that if she had any questions about chemistry, I'd be glad to help her.

Well, she stormed out of my room in a huff mumbling something like "You haven't heard the last of this." Anyway, if this becomes a problem, I would like to have her removed from my class and placed in Bill Sebring's class.

Allen Hackman

High School In-Basket Item #10

To: Dr. Smith <jsmith@htschool.k12.edu>

From: E. Mayhem <emayhem@htschool.k12.edu>

Re: Upset girl

Date: October 21

This morning when I got to my desk, a group of girls were in the office just chattering a mile a minute. I asked them to slow down and have only one talk at a time. Well, they were all pretty well upset, but finally Faith Easterly talked up and said that the reason they were so upset is that Beverly Stillwell's boyfriend said he would kill any other guy who would ask her out and that Beverly really wanted to go out with other guys.

I may just be pushing the panic button (Mr. Wells said I worried too much), but with something like this, I'd rather be safe than sorry.

Just thought you should know.

Elsie Mayhem, Secretary
Hill Top School

High School In-Basket Item # 11

To: Dr. Smith <jsmith@htschool.k12.edu>

From: A. Walker <awalker@htschool.k12.edu>

Re: Homecoming Dance

Date: October 22

I just found out that the Homecoming Committee is requesting the use of the city field house for the homecoming dance this year. Let me fill you in:

About four years ago, Bob gave them permission to hold the homecoming dance at the city field house and to sell tickets to the general public. Well, when the band began to play, the place became a mob scene, and several students were injured. On top of that, there were numerous fights in the parking lot between some of our illustrious former students who thought they'd come to the dance to scout out a new girlfriend.

Take it from me, there is no reason why the homecoming dance should be held at the city field house. The risk is not worth it.

Audrey Walker, Assistant Principal
Hill Top School

High School In-Basket Item #12

To: Dr. Smith <jsmith@htschool.k12.edu>

From: G. Hartworthy <ghartwor@htschool.12.edu>

Re: Changes to the AP program

Date: October 19

I am aware that the school board will consider a item at its October board meeting to open the AP classes at the Hill Top School for any student, regardless of their ability to meet the criteria we have established for inclusion in the AP programs. As chairman for the Social Studies Department at Hill Top School, I must voice my objection to this item and sincerely hope that you will support the Social Studies Department's position. The idea of AP classes is to have students with exceptional ability challenged to the point that upon successful completion of the AP course they can sit for the exam, score at least a 3 out of 5, and receive college credit for the course. If we permit anyone to take the course, we will wind up watering down the material, not covering as much material, and not getting the depth of learning that we currently have.

To stress my point, in the past five years, only three students of the seventy-five who have gone through our AP Social Studies Program have not scored high enough to receive college credit. If we permit any student who would like to try an AP course to enroll in AP Social Studies, we threaten all that we have worked so hard to build.

Gary Hartworthy, Chair
Social Studies Department
Hill Top School

End of the Year

Background

You are Dr. Smith, and you are completing your first year as principal of Hill Top School. It is May 20, and you have gone to the school on a Saturday morning to check over your mail and telephone messages. You have been out of town since Wednesday evening as the result of a family emergency.

Instructions

1. You will be given sixty minutes to read and take action on all of the In-Basket items presented following the instructions. You are not expected merely to describe what you would do, but to do it. For example, if you decide to write a letter, then compose the letter. If you decide to telephone an individual or have a conference with someone, then outline your objectives, as well as the main points or questions that you would present.
2. Each of the In-Basket items requires action, which you should present on another sheet of paper. Attach the action you develop to the In-Basket item it addresses.
3. Proceed to the In-Basket items.

End-of-the-Year In-Basket Item #1

15 May

Memo

To: Dr. Smith

From: John Tuba

In March I submitted my request to conduct summer band lessons so that it would be placed on the board agenda at the April meeting. In reviewing the minutes from the May board meeting, I noticed that this item has still not been brought to a vote.

Everyone in the community takes great pride in the effort of our students when they see them marching at football games or parades, but the only way this caliber of musician can be maintained requires us to invest in their summer training. It seems as though someone is trying to deliberately stop this program. It is imperative that with only 20 days of school left that a decision be made so that publicity for the program can get to the students.

For the sake of our band—PLEASE HELP!

End-of-the-Year In-Basket Item #2

Telephone Message

For: Dr. Smith

From: Jim Engleman (Channel 12 Live Action News)

Time: 1:15 PM, Thursday

Please call him back ASAP. He is putting together a group of educators to face off against the Society against Thematic Teaching (SATT) and wants you on the panel.

End-of-the-Year In-Basket Item #3

12 May, 1995

Dear Dr. Smith,

    The little woman and I are concerned about our daughter, Sandy, and the poor performance she has turned in on her report card. We all know that girls can't possibly do as well as boys in some subjects, but, come on, she should at least be doing B work in english. What with summer coming on and all, what do you think about us getting her enrolled in a summer school program to bring up them awful grades in math and science and history.

    Please get back to me so as we can make plans for our summer vacation (them fish are biting like crazy, you know). Our number is 367-9353.

                          Sincerely,

                          Johnny Bass

End-of-the-Year In-Basket Item #4

Dr. Smith,

In the past, the Mr. Dorfman [the former principal] distributed a "Closing School" form to all the teachers. This form informed the faculty what they had to turn in, put away, etc., so the summer crew could come by and do repair work and painting. Do you have any plans to do something similar? Would you like to see what was done before? (I have some left over from last year.)

Also, Mr. Dorfman developed a form for teachers to request various repair work to be done to their rooms. I also have examples of this for you if you would like to see them.

Let me know what your plans are, and I will be glad to get things put together.

Herbert Helpful

Secretary

End-of-the-Year In-Basket Item #5

May 19

Dr. Smith, I just received a call from my wife. As you know, she is in the Navy. Well, she is being transferred to another location out of state. She will have to leave in two weeks and, of course, she wants me to go with her. I really hate to leave my job, and I would like to stay until at least the end of the school year, but when I mentioned this to her, she didn't seem too receptive. I'm not sure what I should do. Do you have any advice?

Herbert Helpful
Secretary

End-of-the-Year In-Basket #6

Memorandum

To: Dr. Smith

From: Robert Squirrel, Teacher

Date: 2/4/02

Subject: Harassment

The purpose of this memorandum is to register a formal complaint against Ms. Walker, our assistant principal. This woman has sexually harassed me on numerous occasions, and I want it to stop! She has made remarks about my butt, asked me if I sleep nude, and pinched me on the buttocks on several occasions. Three different times, she propositioned me. Yes, I am a new teacher, but I do not believe I should have to take this kind of abuse! Other teachers have told me that she has done similar things to them. I am concerned about my career. I need your help.

End-of-the-Year In-Basket #7

May 17

Dr. Smith,

I am not sure what I would do about this referral. As you probably know, Billy Bob Morris (the student) is the son of one of the school board members. I have never gotten along with the old man too well (him and me were on rival teams when we were in high school) so I would appreciate it if you would handle this one.

Audrey Walker
Assistant Principal

Hill Top School

Student Discipline Referral Form

Student's Name: *Billy Bob Morris*

Date: *Thursday*

Teacher: *Jack Stilwell*

Problem: *Kid keeps fooling around and is disrespectful to me. I am sick and tired of this kid and I don't want him back in class until he shapes up.*

End-of-the-Year In-Basket Item #8

May 18

Dr. Smith,

For some time now, I have been wanting to bring something to your attention, but my daughter has not wanted me to contact you about the matter. However, I feel now that I must say something, whether my daughter wants me to or not.

You are probably not aware of this, but one of your teachers, a Miss Snow, is dating a high school student, and from what I hear, things have progressed pretty far, if you know what I mean. I think this kind of a situation sets a poor example for students, and it makes it difficult for those of us parents who are trying to set a moral tone in our own families. I know you will want to take a strong stand on this. The talk around town is that this boy already has Miss Snow in trouble, if you know what I mean, and that she is considering an abortion.

Obviously, Miss Snow should not be allowed to continue in her position.

Sincerely,

(Mrs.) Sally Parks

End-of-the-Year In-Basket #9

May 19

Dear Dr. Smith.

   I would like to register formally my objection to the way my daughter has been treated in physical education class. My daughter signed up for weight-lifting training second semester after the school promoted this curriculum change for girls. It has come to my attention that the new football coaches, who are now on campus replacing the present coaches and getting football players ready for summer training, have discontinued the girls' weight-lifting program during fifth period and are using the weight room with *football players only* during this time. It appears to me that my daughter's rights have been violated and that this condition is in violation of Title IX requirements and regulations.

   I expect my daughter to be back in the weight-lifting room Monday afternoon, May 22, 1995, during fifth period physical education class continuing her weight-lifting training. Because of all that is involved in this situation and the possible repercussions, I will not identify myself or my daughter. However, if this matter is not addressed appropriately by Monday as requested, I am prepared to take this to the federal courts.

   THANK YOU for your cooperation.

Hill Top School
123 Top of the Hill Lane
Hill Valley, USA 33333

Appendix H
Case Studies

The New Principal Address

The Setting

You have just been informed that, beginning next week, you will become the principal at Hill Top High School, a small rural high school (grades 9–12) in the middle of the state. The community in which the school is located is comprised of people who can trace their roots to the development of the community some 150 years ago. Most of the people in the community are engaged in either agriculture (small, family-owned farms) or work in the local textile mill, which has been experiencing cutbacks in recent years because of the importation of goods from overseas. The board is comprised of three men and two women, one of whom claims that she alone was responsible for hiring the new superintendent. This person's husband was president of the Hill Top Sports Boosters prior to the hiring of the new superintendent.

The superintendent of the system is in her second year of a three-year contract. She was brought in from outside the system amid a scandal involving receipts from football and basketball games. In her second year, she found that the scandal directly involved the high school principal, and she moved to remove him. Following a lengthy legal battle, the principal plea-bargained to step down as principal, provided he could remain as the driver education teacher for the school. As the driver education teacher, he has been instrumental in keeping "the air stirred up" for the assistant principal, who has served as the interim principal. Although this person was in the running for the position to which you have just been appointed, the superintendent thought it would be best to bring in "some new blood to get the school going again."

Faculty and students have been feeling the effects of the problems with the high school principal. Members of the high school faculty have expressed concern about the looseness of the student discipline, as the assistant has tried to be everyone's friend, students and faculty alike. Faculty members have begun cracking down on students to restore discipline, which led to open student rebellion two weeks ago, with the students walking out of their classes at 11:30 A.M. in protest to the mistreatment they are feeling. In addition, the faculty has been ignoring the requests of the acting principal, saying that they want to be involved in the decision-making process and that they are too busy trying to keep the students in line to complete what they term "busywork" reports.

The Problem

The superintendent will introduce you to the faculty and students at an all-school assembly on Monday morning. Your assignment is to use the information gained on organizational thought, school climate, pupil control ideology, morale building and decision making and develop the address you will present, which will, in fact, set the tone of your administrative tenure.

Two High Schools versus One High School

The Community

Hill Top County is located in the rural South. Residents of Hill Top number approximately 35,000, represented by a 40 percent minority of African Americans and Hispanics and a 60 percent white population. The community is progressive in its support of education and in recruiting new business and industrial prospects. The community contains a popular two-year junior college, an agricultural experiment station, numerous corporate agricultural research facilities, and a living history museum. The Hill Top County community was selected as one of the hundred best communities in the United States in which to live.

The School System

The Hill Top school system has an enrollment of approximately 7,800 students. The schools they attend have the following organizational pattern:

- pre-K through fourth-grade schools
- One pre-K through seventh-grade school
- Two fifth- through seventh-grade middle schools
- One eighth- through ninth-grade junior high school
- One tenth- through twelfth-grade high school.

The buildings are well maintained and attractive. To accommodate the increase in student population over the years, new media centers, additional constructed classrooms, and some portable classrooms were added to several schools.

The local community has been a proponent of a strong educational system, often giving tours of the schools as a selling point to potential business and industrial customers interested in relocating. Curriculum and instructional technologies are current and progressive. Community support and lottery dollars have placed many computers and computer labs in the schools. Each elementary classroom has a minimum of three networked computers attached to a file server that contains a curriculum for math and reading. All schools have satellite dishes and modems for the Internet, and the high school utilizes the Channel 1 technology. The school system and employees have been a unified and stable institution and a point of pride in the community.

The Problem

The Hill Top community has been a fortunate and prosperous community. The location of the community at the crossroads of important transportation routes for the South has attracted several major industries, resulting in a steady increase in population. This continuous increase in the school-age population has begun placing demands on the school system that the present school structures are having difficulties accommodating. Anticipating a growth rate that in the near future would place a severe burden on the present school buildings, the board of education adopted a plan of action.

The board of education, with the assistance of individuals, community groups, and civic organizations, appointed a diverse group of thirty-five members from the community, the board of education, and the schools as a study commission. This study commission was given the charge to study the school system and make recommendations to the school board. The study commission availed themselves of research and experts in the areas of school organization, curriculum, buildings, financial concerns, and growth patterns in formulating their recommendations. Following more than a year-long active and very involved process, the commission made its recommendations to the school board. The commission recommended the following school organization and building plan:

- Four pre-K through second-grade schools
- One pre-K through fifth-grade school
- Three third- through fifth-grade schools (schools converted from one former pre-K through fourth-grade school and the two former middle schools)
- Two sixth- through eighth-grade middle schools (the construction of one new middle school and the renovation of the junior high school as a middle school)

• Two ninth- through twelfth-grade high schools (the construction of one new high school and the renovation of the present high school)

These recommendations were designed to take advantage of the maximum capital outlay funds available from the state, develop a more common grade-level organization to maximize use of instructional resources, form two true middle schools, and place the ninth grade at the high schools, where it is traditionally located.

The commission had the choice of recommending the building of one large or two smaller high schools. One large high school containing the grades ninth through twelfth with the present population would have approximately 2,100 students. Growth predictions increase this number to around 2,500 in a few years and close to 3,000 in ten to fifteen years. After researching the advantages and disadvantages of the large high school versus the small high school and construction costs, the commission recommended two smaller high schools (two high schools containing more than 1,000 students each are not small high schools).

The board of education, after studying the recommendations of the commission, voted unanimously to accept the plan. The board immediately began writing the facilities plan to meet the state's requirements and developing a bond referendum plan for funding. In the first few days and weeks after the board's acceptance, proceedings progressed smoothly. As the realization that the traditions of a one-high-school community were coming to an end, an uneasiness began to develop in the community.

Individuals in the community began to speak out against the two-high-school concept. As plans were developed and implemented for the bond referendum, individual concerns became group concerns. The concerns voiced in the community included the idea that one high school would be for the rich students and one for the poor students and the worry that taxes would be raised to a burdensome level on farmers, elderly community members, and average taxpayers. The cost of operating two high schools, how they would be staffed, and the curriculum offerings were questioned. Much concern was expressed about the fact that the sports teams—especially football—band, and other school activities would drop down in classification and no longer compete against major high schools in the region and state.

As the promotion of the bond referendum was introduced, formal opposition to the plan was organized. The Concerned Citizens Group began organizational meetings, advertised in the local media, and challenged the school board on every issue. The school board was accused of giving false and misleading information on taxes and funding requirements. School officials and administrators were accused of forcing the school board's ideas on teachers during faculty meetings, of promoting the bond referendum during school hours with students, and of using school resources in promotional activities.

As the bond referendum vote approached, the opposition increased the pressure to defeat the board's plan. Critical advertisements and letters in the media attacked the school board, the superintendent, individual school administrators, teachers, and community members supporting the plan. The school board and the Concerned Citizens Group each held conferences on the local television and radio stations to promote their causes.

As the pressure mounted, divisions occurred in the rank and file of school employees. Many teachers as well as noncertified employees began to voice opposition to the school board's plan, and some openly demonstrated support for the opposition. The athletic director and head football coach went on a regional television newscast to voice his opposition to the board's two-high-school plan and his support of current athletic competition. This was followed two days later with a front page story in the local newspaper in which he again voiced his opposition to the plan and his support of current athletic competition.

The quiet, peaceful, harmonious community of Hill Top had become anything but what it once was. Personal attacks and mistrust of neighbors became the rule of the day. Divisions became so great that shopping, business, and social habits changed, based on the position individuals supported. When the voters went to the polls, they rejected the referendum's request for funding for the school improvement projects.

Questions to Begin Discussion

1. When the board of education formulates a facilities plan for the school district, should this plan be supported by the employees of the board?

2. What is the role of First Amendment rights of employees in this situation?

3. Should teachers go public with their disagreements with the board of education?

4. Should the athletic director and head football coach go public in the media to express his opposition to his employer?

5. Do public school employees have an implied duty to support the decisions and policies of their boards of education?

6. What does the research indicate about school size and effectiveness?

7. What is your position on the advantages and disadvantages of one large high school versus two small high schools?

8. What are the advantages and disadvantages of locating the ninth grade in a middle school or junior high school versus locating it in a high school?

Zero Tolerance Fighting Policy

The Policy

The Hill Top County school system has not been spared the severe discipline problems gripping other school systems nationwide. Board of education members, sensing increasing concerns from the community and educators over the frequency and severity of discipline problems, passed a zero tolerance fighting policy. The board of education, in passing this policy, emphasized that all students had a right to a safe and secure school environment conducive to learning. In addition to this policy, security officers were placed in the high school and junior high school.

The board of education specified that the zero tolerance policy would apply only to students in the middle schools, the Junior High and the high school. The policy stated that in the event a fight occurred, the appropriate law enforcement officers would be called and each student involved in the fight would be placed under arrest with no exceptions. The policy would be applied equally to all students in all situations.

The Problem

The zero tolerance policy has been in effect for approximately two years without any noticeable problems. Several fights have occurred, and the students involved were escorted away by law enforcement personnel. As a result of the policy and the security officers in the buildings, fighting in the schools has decreased significantly. This year, an unusual number of fights occurred, especially in the middle schools (grades 5, 6, and 7). On several occasions, very young students from the middle schools, especially minority students, were involved in fights and were arrested by law enforcement officers in accordance with board policy. Prior to the enactment this policy, discipline and order in the middle schools had been a primary concern of school officials and the board of education. Following policy enactment, discipline and order continued to be a concern at the middle schools.

At the October board of education meeting, the Rev. J. D. Faith requested and was granted an opportunity to address the board. The Rev. Faith implored the board to rescind the zero tolerance policy because young boys and girls were being taken to jail, the policy was not being implemented fairly, and the school administrators were not consistent in calling law enforcement officers. The board indicated that it would look into how the policy was being enforced but had no intention of rescinding the policy.

The following day, the front page of the local newspaper carried an article and interview with the Rev. Faith. He charged, in the paper, that decisions to call law enforcement officials was based on race, that young children were being thrown in jail with criminals, and that the real criminals were the school officials. He suggested that they were the ones who should be thrown into jail for the terrible injustices they were inflicting on the young people of the community. The Rev. Faith promised that the fight had just begun and that he would not rest until this unjust policy was removed from the school system.

Possible Discussion Questions

1. What is your position on the use of a zero tolerance fighting policy?

2. Do you believe a zero tolerance fighting policy is an effective deterrent in schools?

3. If you are in favor of a zero tolerance policy, what grade levels do you believe this policy should include?

4. What is your position on the use of law enforcement officers in the zero tolerance fighting policy? What options would you not recommend?

5. Following the charges and concerns leveled by the Rev. Faith, the superintendent has requested each school administrator to prepare a response concerning the policy. What will your response be?

The Pregnant Student Teacher

The Student Teacher

Mary Filmore was a popular college student. As a freshman, Mary was the starting center for the women's basketball team. Mary rapidly became a very popular girl on campus and attended many social functions. Participation in these social functions led to a serious romance with another student, which resulted in the birth of a daughter. Mary left school for one quarter and then returned to complete her basketball career, as well as to obtain her teaching degree.

The School

Hill Top Elementary School is a moderately large elementary school of approximately six hundred students. It is a neighborhood school, with more students walking and riding in family cars to school than riding the bus. The school community is 90 percent white middle class, with 7 percent African American and 3 percent Hispanic students.

The Problem

Mary Filmore had completed her course requirements and was now ready for her student teaching assignment. The college, along with the school district personnel director, assigned Mary Filmore to do her student teaching in the second grade at Hill Top Elementary School. Mary appeared to settle into the student teaching role without too much difficulty. The students liked her, and she was very sociable with the faculty and staff of the school.

Within a couple of weeks, the principal detected a rumor that Mary Filmore was pregnant. He was told that he should observe Ms. Filmore more closely because the evidence was showing. Following casual observation, the principal determined that this was indeed the case. It was determined that Ms. Filmore had been pregnant for some time, and that loose-fitting clothing had previously disguised her condition well.

After making inquiries in many different places, the principal determined several facts about the situation. He learned that Ms. Filmore would be delivering this baby within three weeks of completing her student teaching, if the days had been counted correctly. He also determined that Ms. Filmore was not married and that this would be her second illegitimate child.

As the year progressed and Ms. Filmore's condition became obvious to everyone, concerns began to surface. Teachers in the building as well as parents began expressing concerns about the values, ethics, and especially moral character of Ms. Filmore. Some teachers and parents finally told the principal that they felt this situation was the wrong message to be sending to students and that Ms. Filmore should resign her student teaching duties. Since the superintendent is now aware of this situation, he has asked you to make a full report to him on Monday. You have called a meeting with the university personnel to discuss this matter, and will be consulting with the superintendent following this meeting.

Possible Discussion Questions

1. Should the university (if they had known) have informed the school system that an unmarried pregnant student teacher would be assigned?

2. Should the school and master teacher be aware of the condition of incoming student teachers?

3. Are there moral issues involved here that take precedence over individual rights?

4. Should the student teacher have elected on her own not to attend school during this time?

5. What should the principal tell the staff and faculty about this student teacher?

Appendix I
The Leadership Portfolio

The administrative narrative worksheet

Elementary school leadership
portfolio narrative
Beth Checkovich

Elementary school leadership portfolio
narrative
Richard Campbell

Middle school leadership portfolio narrative
Richard Fletcher

High school leadership portfolio narrative
George Kornegay

Leadership portfolio evaluation criteria

The Leadership Portfolio Narrative Worksheet

This worksheet has been designed to help you get started on the important narrative section of your leadership portfolio. Describe your accomplishments and give examples, where appropriate, to further illustrate your responses.

1. Describe your past teaching responsibilities.

2. Describe your teaching methods and explain *why* you teach as you do. (Particular attention should be given to strategy and implementation.) Provide examples.

3. Describe course projects, class assignments, or other activities that have helped you integrate your subject matter with your students' outside experiences.

4. Describe any administrative responsibilities you have had within the past five years.

5. Describe techniques you use in school leadership, and explain why you lead in this particular manner. Give examples.

6. Describe specific leadership activities that help you relate to certified and noncertified personnel, students, and parents.

7. If you overheard teachers talking about you and your leadership style in the teachers' lounge, what would they probably be saying? What would you like them to say? Why is that important to you?

8. If you overheard students talking about you and your leadership style in the cafeteria, what would they probably be saying? What would you like them to say? Why is that important to you?

9. Give examples and describe specific ways that you motivate certified and noncertified employees to help them achieve better performance.

10. Give examples and describe specific ways that you motivate students to help them achieve better performance.

11. Describe your efforts to develop your leadership effectiveness.
    a. Workshops and conferences Attended

    b. Informal assessment of your own leadership style

    c. Describe your presentations and publications on teaching and
        administration.

12. How do you stay current in leadership? How do you translate this
    new knowledge into your leadership activities?

Beth Checkovich
Elementary School Leadership Portfolio Narrative

Narrative

- Introduction
- Teaching and Learning Philosophy
- Teaching Responsibilities
- Teaching Methods
- Leadership Philosophy
- Administrative Responsibilities
- Leadership Activities
- Interactions with the Community
- Human and Public Relations
- Assessment of Effectiveness
- Awards and Recognitions
- Grants and Publications
- Professional Development Activities
- Future Leadership Goals and Directions

Appendices

(Varies according to model selected)

Introduction

An introduction is a polite way to meet others. Therefore, I would like to introduce myself to you. My name is Beth H. Young Checkovich. Born a Pennsylvanian, I have lived in Virginia for the last 37 years and in Winchester, Virginia, for 21 of those years. I am married to Dr. Peter G. Checkovich who is the Provost of the Shepherd Community and Technical College in Shepherdstown, West Virginia, and I have two exceptional daughters, Holly and Stephanie. Holly will soon graduate from the McIntire School of Commerce at the University of Virginia with a B.S. in Accounting. Stephanie is finishing her second year at Mary Washington College in Fredericksburg. In April, I was notified by

George Mason University that I was accepted into the Ed.D. in Education program and will begin part-time coursework this fall. I am also participating in the Principal Preparation Program through George Mason, for which I will receive a certificate and an endorsement by the fall of 1999. More information regarding my work experience and education can be found on my resume in appendix M.

Teaching and Learning Philosophy

I believe every child can be successful whether they are visual, kinesthetic, or auditory learners. My responsibility is to meet my students' educational needs. I must search for appropriate resources so students can be instructed at their cognitive level. Through many opportunities, including hands-on, lecture, questioning, writing, reading, problem solving, research, experimentation, observation, discussion, games, and projects, I want students to explore and learn about a variety of topics. I believe students need many hands-on experiences to help them learn a topic, remember important concepts, and use that knowledge in new or in real-life situations where they can be successful both in and outside of school. Teaching is helping students "to learn how to do something" so the "knowledge, insight" is relevant and meaningful to them.

A teacher should be a diagnostician. As the professional, I must know my students' strengths and weaknesses to help them achieve better in school. Included in this diagnosis is assessment. If I am successful in my efforts, students will learn. Otherwise, I must modify my program so I can better reach the needs of my students.

Motivating students is also important. Because of my enthusiasm and interest in learning, students will care about education. However, teaching is not just a job or presenting facts, but an opportunity to show students that someone cares about them because everyone deserves to be cared about by an adult.

Listening to the needs of my students and their parents, my colleagues, my administrators, my community, and myself is a critical aspect of teaching. Through listening, I am able to analyze situations better and make effective decisions.

Finally, I believe in accepting change because nothing in education is static. There are dynamic educational changes occurring daily, especially with curriculum standards and technology. I need to be prepared to face these changes and make wise decisions regarding their implementation.

Teaching Responsibilities

For the last nine years I have taught at Middletown Elementary School. In my first year, I taught third grade, and for the remaining eight years, I have taught fifth grade. Most of these positions have been teaching regular education students; however, I did teach alternative education classes (students below the 25th percentile) for three years.

This year I am teaming with a colleague and have the responsibility of teaching two science classes, two math classes, and two spelling classes, along with managing my home base class (see appendix A).

While teaching is the most important aspect of my daily routine, I am also responsible for planning lessons, grading that includes informal and formal assessments, and discipline. Some examples of the assessments and process skills worksheets I have written are included in appendix A.

Part of the responsibilities of a teacher is to make sure all tasks have been completed well. Not only should routine assignments such as report cards be interesting to read, but some students should also find daily activities interesting and fun (see appendix A). I believe teachers should strive to have a positive, motivating environment in their classroom.

Additional responsibilities I have are to attend meetings. These meetings may be faculty meetings or meetings with students, parents, or administrators (see appendix A). Finally, I am responsible for any cocurricular activities I agree to do or have been told to do by my school administrator or central office administrator.

One meeting that I regularly attend is that of the county-level Science Curriculum Committee. This committee is responsible for the direction of elementary science in all ten elementary schools in the county. Our greatest accomplishment to date is the countywide Science Curriculum Guide included in appendix A.

Teaching Methods

There are three main teaching methods I try to incorporate daily. I vary the methods frequently to keep interest in the content high and to meet as many learning needs of my students as possible.

First, I teach with a visual strategy. I like to show examples of real content matter scattered throughout the classroom. There are many posters and bulletin boards that can help students remember content information. Much guided practice is given that allows me to make a quick assessment of the students and how much additional practice they need before they can do independent work. I also teach visually through modeling. If I show my students exactly what I want something to look like, then I can expect some students to equal or surpass that ideal and other students to try to reach some part of that expectation (see appendix B).

Second, I teach through questioning techniques. Asking many questions keeps the students' attention and checks their understanding of the material as we are learning about it. Fast, informal assessments can be made easily through questioning.

Finally, I teach with many hands-on activities. Having many practice sessions will guarantee more successful learning. This practice helps to bridge the transition between concrete work and abstract knowledge. Hands-on activities also help students develop higher level thinking skills that are necessary for problem solving. Photographs of students engaged in these activities are included in appendix B.

It is not always easy for students to understand concepts, even after hands-on work. For this reason, many opportunities are given to the students to explore simple concepts. Eventually, I move them toward more complex topics as they appear ready.

Leadership Philosophy

I believe in being a leader who is visible to those around her. Therefore, managing by walking around rather than remaining in the office throughout the day is extremely important. A leader needs to be aware of the role each member of the staff plays and should participate in that role at least once throughout the year. It would be difficult to be critical of another individual if I did not have some idea of what kind of job they had.

A fair leader is essential in an organization. She must allow everyone the opportunity to grow if they desire that opportunity. A leader must be sociable, have a caring and positive demeanor, and yet be strong enough to handle the criticisms and anger that are inevitable with the position. Handling stress is critical in a leadership role.

Giving encouragement and having the drive to meet high expectations are leadership skills all leaders must have. Time must be spent wisely by the staff. A leader must make sure there are results after decisions have been made. Achievement must be seen, not just heard.

Keeping up to date with current trends in education, especially in curriculum and technology, is a necessary skill for any leader. Knowing everything would be impossible for a leader, but at least she could enlist the help of those on her staff who are specialists in a curricular area to keep her and other staff members aware of the current trends, issues, and changes.

A participative management style as explained by Max DePree in *Leadership Is an Art* should be especially appealing to a leader. Everyone on the staff is able to participate in making decisions, but the final decisions, the final votes, are made by those who will be most affected by the decision, not by everyone on the staff. The leader must take the final responsibility for any decision made, yet she must trust those on her staff to be capable adults who need to be given room to grow as leaders with their own strengths.

Finally, I believe a leader must have a vision. That vision is what will move the school forward. With a solid vision and a successful, positive environment in which maximum learning can take place, a leader can ensure the effectiveness of her school.

Administrative Responsibilities

The most important administrative responsibility I have is being the science lead teacher for Middletown Elementary School. In this position, I coordinate the math/science family night. I conduct science in-services and meet with faculty to plan hands-on science lessons.

Also, I inventory, purchase, and store science equipment for the school. Another administrative responsibility I have had in the past has been the team leader of the fifth grade. In this position, I attended monthly meetings with the principal, planned and led weekly meetings of the team, completed field trip permission forms, and served as the liaison between the administration and the fifth-grade staff.

A third administrative responsibility has been being a mentor for new faculty on the team. As a mentor, I explain procedures and answer questions and generally guide the new staff member into understanding what Middletown Elementary School does on a daily basis and what is required of all staff. A final responsibility has been being a student teacher supervisor for a college student entering the education field. In one situation, I was shadowed by a college student who visited each week for at least an hour throughout one semester. In another situation, I shared my classroom with a student who was in her last semester at college. I discussed the role of a teacher especially during the first year, explained procedures, reviewed her lesson plans, and critiqued her teaching to help her improve her teaching skills.

Leadership Activities

One of the most important leadership activities in which I have been involved is being the coordinator for the annual math/science family night. Individual students and classes make science fair projects that are on display throughout the night. A plethora of science- and math-related activities fill the cafeteria, gymnasium, and hallways, encouraging children and their parents to interact while doing something related to math or science. Several documents showing the information that is distributed to parents, students, and staff for math/science family night are enclosed in appendix D.

For the first time this year, I introduced a computer family night. Fifteen students were invited to spend several hours at school with their parents working in the computer lab on the computer game Amazon Trail. We had a pizza dinner, played medicine ball in the gym, and spent at least two and a half hours working in the lab (see appendix D).

Two years ago, a first-grade teacher and I sponsored parent workshops held one hour before the general PTA meetings. Many parents were appreciative of the information they received during these workshops (see pictures in appendix D).

School-related leadership activities focus on leading faculty professional development activities in science, math, and technology (see appendix C). I have learned more about the subjects I studied because I had to teach them to others. Self-confidence builds and content knowledge increases when you are present at an in-service offering with your faculty. I continue to evaluate and improve my in-service presentations frequently to make sure the faculty gain as much information and skill as possible. In-service activities I have conducted for Middletown Elementary School faculty include:

Cooperative Discipline (1992)
Science Curriculum (1993)
Math Curriculum (1994)
Science V-Quest Activities (1994–1996), including Math/Science
    Materials Tea
Math Metric Olympics
Va PEN Sign-Up Day
Experimental Design and the Four-Question Strategy
Math/Science Family Night
Earth Day School-Wide Celebration
Individual grade-level professional development
Using Technology (1997);

A professional development activity for district administration staff on using laser disk technology was held in 1996. Also this year, I held an in-service for Redbud Run and Robinson Elementary School faculty at Redbud Run Elementary School on experimental design and the four-question strategy. Following my V-Quest training, I conducted a staff training session on experimental design for teachers at Boyce Elementary School in Clarke County.

One unique feature in my classroom is a menagerie of animals, including a snake, a tarantula, a gerbil, and fish. To help second-grade classes with their study of spiders, I conduct an annual Spider and Snake program for all the second grade classes. In 1995, I organized a school-wide Earth Day celebration which included speakers and activities.

Other leadership activities have included committee work for Frederick County and the State of Virginia. I participated in the Technology Planning Committee that wrote the Technology Plan, a six-year guide for the direction of technology in Frederick County (see appendix D). Also in 1996, 1 was selected to serve on the State Standard Objectives of Learning Science Assessment Committee. We were charged with the responsibility of selecting test items for the State SOL Science Test given to all third-graders throughout the state of Virginia.

Interactions with the Community

A conscious commitment to my community and to the parents and students in my school has been and continues to be one of my primary goals. As a result, I have organized science fairs and math/science family nights to encourage parents' participation in their child's education (see appendix D). I coplanned and presented three parent workshops that were offered to any parent prior to our monthly PTA meetings (see appendix D).

A second area of community commitment is through Alpha Delta Kappa, an international honorary sorority for women educators, in which I have been a charter member and president (see appendix E). I have volunteered for the Youth Development Center by chaperoning dances, the Shelter for Abused Women, Doo-Dah Day, a celebration sponsored by the Child-Parent Center, and the Creative Arts Festival. I have also contributed time and money to fund-raisers that enable ADK to offer a scholarship to an education major at the local university and to give money to help charitable organizations in the community and to purchase instructional materials for schools.

A third area of community commitment is through local professional memberships. It is vital for teachers to become involved in professional development to remain current with educational trends and to develop relationships with area professionals sharing similar interests. As a result of my membership in the National Science Teachers Association and the Virginia Association of Science Teachers (VAST), I felt it would be beneficial to have a regional science teachers' group in this area. In 1994, 1 contacted several colleagues to generate interest in creating this regional group that would be affiliated with VAST. In November, the NorthWest Association of Science Teachers (NoWASTe) was born. We have much to accomplish to promote science education throughout the area and between science educators from the elementary to the collegiate levels, but we have high expectations (see appendix E).

As a member of the Education Committee of the Shenandoah Discovery Museum, I am able to promote and support science education in the community. Previous community work has included volunteering for the Apple Blossom Festival and being a Sunday school teacher, a vacation Bible school teacher, a Girl Scout leader, and a community arts program instructor. I have participated in the Parent-Teacher organizations for my daughters' schools and in several activities for the high school athletic association and senior class. I also taught a summer youth enrichment course, Mix It Up with Science, at Lord Fairfax Community College. It is impossible to be involved in education without including community activities. See my resume in appendix K for a listing of all professional and community organizations to which I currently belong.

In the professional community, I have been asked to demonstrate lessons to local teachers who want to see hands-on science being taught. Showing interested teachers how to incorporate science activities in their lessons is the best way I can promote science education locally.

To remain current with educational trends and issues, I regularly read professional journals such as *Educational Leadership, Science and Children, Mailbox,* and publications from professional organizations to which I belong. Currently, I belong to NoWASTe (NorthWest Association of Science Teachers), VAST (Virginia Association of Science Teachers), NSTA (National Science Teachers Association), ASCD (Association for School Curriculum Development), AVRC (Apple Valley Reading Council), VSRA (Virginia State Reading Association), FCEA (Frederick County Education Association), VEA (Virginia Education Association), NEA (National Education Association), and PDK (Phi Delta Kappa). Involvement in these organizations varies, depending on my available time. However, it is important to develop a network of individuals who share similar interests and whom you may contact and use their skills or knowledge if necessary.

Human and Public Relations

Sending letters to staff members and parents for their participation in different events or projects is one way I try to show appreciation for their efforts. Communication is important for teachers. Parents need to be contacted regarding field trips or upcoming events. Logical, accurate letter-writing skills demonstrate the high standards teachers must have when communicating (see appendix F). Additionally, when speaking to parents, such as at the fifth-grade awards night, it is important to be clear, concise, and positive (see appendix F).

Assessment of Effectiveness

Attending workshops and conferences is one way to develop your effectiveness as a leader (see appendix G). Workshops or conferences I have attended throughout my career include:

Mathematics Unlimited
Whole Language
Peer Pressure Reversal
Hurray for Books
Learning Styles
Experimental Design
Virginia State Reading Association Conference
Improving the Fifth-Grade Curriculum
Virginia Association of Science Teachers Conference
National Science Teachers Association Conference
Joint Math/Science Conference
V-Quest Conference (2 years)
V-Quest Workshops
Regional Social Studies Conference
Math Their Way of Thinking
Heath Math Curriculum
Project WILD

SEARCH Conference
Cooperative Discipline
Virginia Agriculture in the Classroom
Focus on Change Conference
Environmental Education
Shenandoah National Park Teacher Training
Technology
AIMS (1996)
National Teacher Training Institute
National Storytelling Festival (1997)

In 1995 and 1996, I made presentations at two science conferences and one children's literature conference. Watch Yeast Expand Your Teaching, an experimental design workshop using yeast, was presented in 1995 for Virginia's First Joint Conference on Teaching Math and Science. My second presentation, Mix It Up with Science, an experimental design workshop on matter and mixtures, was given in 1996 for the Virginia Association of Science Teachers. A third presentation was on teaching science with literature and included an activity on adopting a schoolyard tree (see appendix G).

Awards and Recognition

In August 1994, I was given the highest honor awarded to a teacher. I was selected to be the Frederick County Teacher of the Year for 1995–1996 (see appendix H). Letters from the community regarding these recognitions can be found in appendix L. This award has been so meaningful because it acknowledges the efforts I have put into the work of which I am most proud. I was also chosen Middletown Elementary School Teacher of the Year for 1994–1995, after being on the ballot for three previous years (see appendix H).

At the VAST 1996 conference, I was awarded the 1996 VAST Award for Outstanding Contribution to Science Education in Virginia at the Elementary Level (see appendix H). This award was a complete surprise and again represents one of the highest honors I could achieve, especially when it was given to me by other science educators in the state.

In 1992, I was chosen to receive the Alpha Delta Kappa Scholarship for Graduate Studies. Also, from 1993 to the present, I was selected to represent Middletown Elementary School as the V-Quest science lead teacher. Presenting at conferences has been a tremendous recognition as well.

Grants and Publications

Teachers need help with funding special projects that are not included as part of a school's budget. I had written and submitted several proposals for grants and received three.

1. Recipient of a 1997 Frederick County Educational Foundation Grant (purchasing an accelerated reader computer program for the school)
2. Recipient of a 1997 Virginia Commission for the Arts Technical Assistance Grant (to have an artist instruct teachers on art techniques, resulting in better science observations, which can then be taught to students; see appendix K)
3. Recipient of a 1996 Frederick County Educational Foundation Grant (purchasing an instant camera to record science experiments)

Publishing is not an area in which all teachers need to participate. However, I enjoy writing when I have time and have been rewarded in having several articles published.

1. Article published in *Learningworks, Newsletter for West Virginia Educators* (see appendix K)
   A poem published in *Voices from Virginia*, a Virginia Alpha Delta Kappa booklet.
   Two articles and a letter to the editor published in the local newspaper
   For a teachers as researcher graduate class, my research on science education methods was published

Professional Development Activities

Of all the possible improvement activities, the most important one is being able to continue my education. Although I am involved in organizations, attend workshops and conferences, participate on county and state curricular committees, and belong to several professional groups, I believe I understand educational theories and practices more comprehensively as a result of taking classes. Certainly my abilities as a teacher and leader have improved. Recommendation letters from my principal to begin educational programs are quite complimentary and encourage me to continue striving to do the best I can do (see appendix J). Graduate classes I have taken so far include:

School Administration, Spring 1998, GMU

Research in Language and Learning (Teachers as Researchers), Fall 1996, Shenandoah University

Introduction to Instructional Supervision, Summer 1996, UVA

Advanced Curriculum and Instruction: Integrating Math and Science, Spring 1995, Virginia Tech

Adolescent Development, Fall 1994, Virginia Tech

Statistics in Behavioral Science, Summer 1994, Virginia Tech

Foundations of Educational Research and Evaluation, Summer 1994, Virginia Tech

Advanced Educational Psychology, Summer 1994, Virginia Tech

Middle School Curriculum, Spring 1994, Virginia Tech

Foundations of Reading, Fall 1993, JMLI

Elementary School Curriculum, Summer 1993, JMU

Elementary Reading Program, Summer 1993, JMU

Organizing for Effective Literature Instruction, Summer 1993, JMLI

Cooperative Learning, Fall 1992, JMU

Activity Based Science Instruction, Fall 1991, JMLI

BRIES, the Blue Ridge Institute for Environmental Studies, Summer 1991, Shenandoah University

Assertive Discipline, Spring 1990, Shenandoah University

Teaching in Discipline and Classroom Management, Fall 1988, JMU

Workshop in Education, Summer 1988, GMU

Future Leadership Goals and Directions

As early as thirteen years ago, when I began my career in education, I reflected on where I wanted to be in the future. Several directions were known: I wanted to be an educator in the public school system, and I wanted to teach science. As my career continued, I enjoyed taking graduate classes and attending professional workshops and conferences. I also enjoyed bringing back information I thought would be helpful to my colleagues and sharing it with them. A plan for my future was beginning to develop.

Focusing on my areas of interest and activities I enjoyed doing, I realized that pursuing both a certificate in educational leadership and a doctorate in science education leadership would best meet my needs as a professional. In the spring I was accepted into the Ed.D. program George Mason University, helping me to realize my dream. I do not take this goal lightly. Although I have worked very hard in my career so far, I know it will take even more effort to achieve my plans. My creativity, initiative, and desire to learn prove that I am ready and eager to meet the challenge (see appendix J).

While I am working toward my Ed.D., I know I want to continue working with other teachers and adults as well as children. To be in that position would require an educational leadership certificate that would qualify me to be an assistant principal and eventually a principal. In this role I can make an educational impact on the community in which I teach. I would be able to share instructional ideas with faculty and encourage an atmosphere of academic pondering as new research is uncovered and discussed. By working with students and their parents, I can help them make plans for greater success in school. Both statistical information and teacher input can assist in this effort. As an educational leader, I would be able to contact community leaders to increase the involvement of the community within the school. Writing grant proposals would help to bring in speakers and businesses to talk to students and to help with materials and projects that could be of benefit to the school, students, families, and the community. So many opportunities could become available if I had the proper academic qualifications and if the position became available.

With my background and interest in curriculum and development, science, technology, and research, I want work on research in science education that is needed in education. Eventually, I would be able to play a more vital role in the development of science education as a science supervisor or curriculum specialist. This role would not be available unless I was a building-level manager first. I need to understand how the individual school works and operates and how the teachers respond to suggestions and change before I can be in a more supervisory role at the district level.

In the future, I also want to conduct research that could benefit future generations of teachers and students. Educators need to be encouraged to be creative in their classrooms and to generate new ideas. However, research is needed to determine if the idea is being successful. Before state- or district-wide curriculum adoptions or deletions are made, such as whole language, research must be conducted.

The future has so much promise. The possibility of continuing my education is very exciting, but so is the idea of being in a position where I can suggest and implement ideas that can impact the future by working with teachers and parents. Having an educational leadership certificate and eventually a doctorate in science education leadership may provide the opportunity for our school district to incorporate a full-time science curriculum specialist. This specialist would be someone who, by having been a principal, understands the intimate workings of a school and who could be a vital resource to all the elementary teachers in our district. I am eager to begin working toward this goal.

Richard Campbell
Elementary School Leadership Portfolio Narrative

Narrative

Leadership Philosophy
Teaching and Learning Philosophy
Administrative Responsibilities
Analysis of Leadership Techniques, Strategies
Description of Leadership Practices
Assessment of Effectiveness
Awards and Recognition
Improvement Activities
Future Leadership Goals/ Directions

Appendices

(According to model selected: NCATE, NPBEA, or ISSLIC)

Leadership Philosophy

Leadership is a process of giving meaningful direction to mutual effort, and causing willing effort to be given to accomplish purpose. It is a social influence process where intentional influence is exerted by one person over other people to structure the activities and relationships in a group or organization. I believe leadership is a group role where the leader can exert real leadership through effective participation in groups. The leader depends upon the frequency of interaction with the followers. As a leader, I must conceptualize tasks and communicate the approach to those tasks to others in the organization. The pattern of task identification and response forms the basis of an operating theory.

I feel the leader often deals with tasks that are not permanent solutions to needs. In such cases, the way in which people, resources, and ideas are organized is the responsibility of the leader. The leader must be capable of structuring the organization and work environment that can respond to those needs. I think working with a diverse group of individuals with different needs and perceptions, the leader must set standards and other expectations that will affect the resolution of problems. These standards may include work habits, communication procedures, time limitations, and a host of related planning areas.

My feeling is that persons assigned to leadership positions generally must structure organizations by suggesting changes and initiating policies. One important task for a leader is using such authority to establish a desirable work climate. Such a climate is made up of the collective perceptions of persons affected by the structure of the organization Leadership is a product of human exchanges or transactions within the organization. It is essential that interpersonal relationships contribute to the attainment of desired ends. The way in which a leader interacts with others in the organization can assist in interpersonal relationships.

Teaching and Learning Philosophy

Teaching requires that the individual providing instruction has knowledge and information that the learner does not have and that the teacher has specialized skill necessary to impart that important information to the learner. The methodology varies based on the composition or learning styles of the class and the objectives of the content. A good teacher must accomplish many tasks at the same time. One such task is leadership through classroom management and organization. This is a crucial function that must be carried out daily during every aspect of the instructional process.

Another task includes preparation for instruction that requires such things as the completion of lesson plans for students. These plans provide a guide for leading the students where the teacher would have them go in learning. One other example is the frequency in assessing student progress. This provides much needed feedback in ensuring that students who need remediation receive it and that those who do not are able to move on.

It is important for educators to understand how students learn. This provides the basis for decisions made to provide the best possible instruction. The knowledge gained by the study of processing information makes teachers aware that for students to learn, one must have their attention. If the information provided is not received by the sensory receptors, it cannot become a part of the learner's short-term memory. Such information may be provided but is lost to the student.

Maintaining the interest of the child helps to ensure that students commit the material to their short-term memory. Having accomplished this, the instructor can then provide the activities necessary for practice. These activities allow students to add this information to their memory. Information then becomes available for use whenever the student needs it.

I think each learner should be allowed an educational opportunity that gives them a chance to reach their potential. Since the school exists for the learner, every effort must be made to ensure adequate instruction for every child who enters the doors of the institution. The learner is a unique, free choosing, and responsible individual made up of intellect and emotion. Education allows for the needs of man when it inculcates the child with certain essential skills and knowledge that all men should possess.

Administrative Responsibilities

I have performed a number of administrative duties while employed by the county school system. The duty that I am best known for is that of school reporter for the system newsletter. It is my responsibility to gather newsworthy information at the school and compile it for the monthly publication (see appendix F). This task requires me to keep abreast of occurrences throughout the school. The items reported include all employees and students. With this responsibility comes the task of obtaining releases for all individuals photographed that are to appear in the publication.

Another task that I perform is in the area of emergency preparedness. As coordinator of the emergency management team for the elementary school, I am charged with the duty of modifying and updating the emergency plan for the school yearly (see appendix D) . I also provide in-service training during preplanning each year as mandated by the state regarding the emergency plan (see appendix H) This responsibility requires that I serve on the school system's emergency management team. The system team deals with the issue of management for all the schools in the county. As a member, I was involved in the implementation of the plan for the entire system (see appendix D). Other duties performed include regular inspections of the facilities, radiological monitoring, preparing school-level exercises, and keeping current evacuation plans.

A fulfilling task that I perform yearly is the campaign for the nonprofit organizations in our community. As a school system member of the Organized Volunteer Effort, my responsibility is to collect money for the American Cancer Society, the American Heart Association, and the United Way (see appendix B). In performing this task, I acquaint the employees with the program during a faculty meeting and pass out information. Then, over the next two-week period, I go to each individual and collect their contributions. I find that by seeing each person in this way, it adds a personal aspect to collecting. After all contributions are made, I complete the school contribution forms. I then compile and balance totals, turning them in to be used as a part of the system totals.

While serving as community relations coordinator for the elementary school, one task I perform involves submitting the honor roll for publication in the local newspaper (see appendix F). This requires obtaining from teachers the names of third-, fourth-, and fifth-grade students making the honor roll. After receiving a list for each grade level, I alphabetize them and prepare them for copy. They are then delivered for publication. At the conclusion of each year, I compile a list of students achieving honor roll for the year to be recognized during Honors Day by the Parent-Teacher Organization.

Star Lab provided yet another opportunity for me to perform administrative tasks (see appendix G). I am charged with obtaining dates for the lab to be used at the school. I am also required to arrange for the unit after it arrives. Once there, students in all grades must have access to it. I am responsible for organizing a schedule to be used for this purpose. The materials necessary for instructions accompanying the labs are then evaluated, as well as the equipment. In addition, I make several lesson presentations. At the conclusion of time allocated for use at the school, my tasks involves disassembly and preparation for pickup.

Analysis of Leadership Techniques, Strategies

The techniques I have used in school leadership have currently been limited to influence tactics. The primary reason is that there is no chance at all to use the power approach. I am not in a position to employ this approach since I am not in an administrative position. There is no threat of any act that I can use to require individuals to perform tasks.

A behavior tactic I have employed often is rational persuasion. In coordinating the drive to collect contributions for charitable organizations, I've had to use logical arguments to support the reasons employees should contribute. This helps to make the request viable and usually results in receiving desired contributions.

Personal appeal is a tactic frequently used as well. In performing tasks it is sometimes necessary to appeal to feelings of loyalty and friendship toward me when requesting something. An example would be in requesting volunteers to serve at the local mall during the education fair (see appendix F). When asked, those who feel close to me will ultimately be the first to offer assistance because they are likely to hope for my success.

Description of Leadership Practices

In my very limited capacity as a leader, there are a few practices that I feel are worthy of applying at this stage of my development. First, as a leader, it is helpful to know who is in your charge. This knowledge is helpful in providing the basis for establishing expectations. I would never ask any employee to perform a task that I myself would not be willing to do. Second, I have a need to understand fully the situation I'm involved in. Before influencing a situation, it is important for me to make certain the change will be positive. Considering all possible ramifications is important to me. Next, I feel that flexibility is necessary. My ability to adjust to the situation is one of my finest qualities. Finally, I feel that the ability to communicate is crucial. If one has vision and cannot communicate it, no true vision exists.

Assessment of Effectiveness

I feel that leader effectiveness is the extent to which the leader's organizational unit performs its task successfully and attains its goal.

The attitude of the followers toward the leader is a common indicator of leader effectiveness. Objective measures of behavior, such as absenteeism, voluntary turnover, grievances, complaints to higher management, requests for transfer, and work slowdowns, serve as indirect indicators of follower dissatisfaction. They may even indicate hostility toward the leader. I believe the leader's contribution to the quality of group process can be used to assess leader effectiveness also.

Awards and Recognition

In my professional career, I have been the recipient of several awards. In 1986, I was named Teacher of the Year for Pine Grove Elementary School (see appendix M), and 1991 marks the year I received the Honors Day award for faculty recognition (see appendix M). In January of 1995, I received recognition by the Lowndes County Board of Education for being selected employee of the month for January (see appendix M).

Improvement Activities

The elementary school where I am employed has in place two programs designed to foster appropriate behavior in the school environment. The first is the T.A.P. (Think! Act Positively) program. This program rewards students for appropriate behavior. Each student is assigned a team based on the colors of the rainbow. The members of that team earn tokens based on application of proper behavior. Each time an employee notices a child displaying proper behavior, the student receives a token. The behavior can range from helping a peer by picking up a book that was dropped to walking away to avoid a fight. At the end of the six-week period, the team with the most token wins a T.A.P. party. Students displaying improper behavior receive T.A.P. slips. Three slips during the course of any week result in assignment to T.A.P. class. This class is for after-school detention. Children are required to reflect on the inappropriate behavior they have displayed.

The second program involves peer mediation (see appendix E). Conflict Managers are trained in the art of helping their peers resolve their differences in a positive way. When disputes arise, students can choose to have a mediator work with them to solve the problem. Those choosing to have the matter settled by the teacher still have that option.

Our school improvement activities were centered around the selection and training of these conflict managers. The first task involved identifying potential candidates for the 1995–1996 school year. This was accomplished by first explaining the program to the fourth-grade students and then, based on the criteria, having them vote for three people in their class that they felt would do a good job. After all students had voted, we determined winners from each class and listed them as potential managers. The next step involved conferring with their teachers to determine whether they felt favorable concerning the selection. If the teacher confirmed, we accepted that student as a manager.

Notification was then given to parents with a request for permission for their child to participate. Obtaining this permission from the parents, we then scheduled training sessions for students (see appendix E). Once the sessions were completed, we assigned future managers to current managers to allow them to observe the strategy . In addition to training, we assessed the effectiveness of the program. Researching the topic, we found an instrument we could use to evaluate the program. We reproduced the instrument and provided students and teachers a chance to respond to items related to their feelings about the program. There was also an instrument to be completed by the managers (see appendix E).

Future Administrative Goals/Directions

My immediate goals are to seek employment in the area of leadership and meet the requirements for enrollment in the six-year program at State University. I hope to ascend to the role of principal, and my desire is to make a difference in the lives of children. It is my hope that I can use the information available on effective schools to create that environment in my school.

Richard Fletcher
Middle School Leadership Portfolio Narrative

Table of Contents

Narrative

Leadership Practices

When I function as a leader within my school, I usually operate in a democratic way. I also try to move around the building and communicate with all faculty involved face to face. When the eighth-grade team has a decision to make, I discuss the situation and all appropriate decisions with my team members, whether that is in a team meeting or I circulate to all of these teachers during my planning period. Prior to language arts curriculum meetings, I meet individually with all committee members to review the agenda with them and to solicit their advice on other topics to include on the agenda. In all leadership situations, I believe involving all members, encouraging shared decision making, and communicating with these members on a one-to-one basis is essential for my success as a leader. I also believe that recognizing the accomplishments of my team or committee members is important for gaining their respect and support (see appendix J).

In all leadership situations, both in and out of the classroom, I act as a role model for those around me. I demonstrate effective time management, goal setting, fairness, and organizational skills, and I always work just as hard as those around me. I feel this has benefited me as a leader because I have gained the support and dedication of those around me.

Administrative Responsibilities

My administrative duties have included language arts committee chairperson, eighth-grade discipline manager, representative on the superintendent's committee on the county middle school grading policy, field trip coordinator, curriculum development, athletic management, and eighth-grade team leader.

As chairperson of the language arts committee, I am responsible for setting meeting dates, meeting individually with committee members before the meeting to establish concerns and topics for discussion, setting the agenda prior to the meeting, communicating meeting times and agendas to the administration, and providing each grade-level team in the building with minutes of the meetings. I am also responsible for coordinating the development of a building-wide syllabus for language arts at each grade level. The language arts committee will provide this document to all parents at the beginning of each school year. In addition to my in-school language arts responsibilities, I will also serve as a representative on the 1998 Virginia State Instructional Materials Review Committee (see appendix A).

When I served as eighth-grade discipline manager, I was responsible for developing a discipline plan for the team (see appendix D). I was also responsible for the management of student records and for communication with the team, the administration, and the parents. I kept up-to-date files on all students, coordinated team meetings with students, discussed team concerns with parents, organized parent conferences, and communicated relevant concerns to the students' other teachers (related arts and PE). When the administration needed team information to make administrative decisions, I met with them to review student files, team meetings, and parent contacts.

My duties as field trip coordinator included planning and implementing field trips to Washington, D.C., for over a hundred students. I was responsible for developing the entire trip, including scheduling buses, contacting museums, coordinating chaperones, providing parents and administration with all plans and the itinerary, and collecting money. On the day of the trip, I was responsible for designating bus assignments, briefing parent chaperones before the trip, communicating all plans with the bus drivers, providing medicine kits and last-minute plans to chaperones, and monitoring student attendance each time we loaded and unloaded the buses (see appendix F).

When Shenandoah County decided to change the middle school grading policy, I served as a school representative on the super-intendent's committee. In this capacity I was responsible for compiling concerns and suggestions within my building, reporting these ideas to the superintendent and other members of the committee, discussing countywide suggestions with the committee members, and reporting the results to the teachers in my building. The committee also assisted in drafting a document to present to the school board (appendix A).

My responsibilities with school curriculum have included the development and implementation of schoolwide curricular and extracurricular programs. I have served on a committee of eight teachers and an administrator to develop and implement a schoolwide interdisciplinary unit for Appalachia Educational Laboratories. I coordinated an effort within my school's language arts program to develop a cohesive language arts curriculum for grades five through eight. In addition, I have developed and organized two activity programs that ran during Friday study hall periods (see appendices A and L).

While serving as a coach at the middle school level, I developed and maintained an organized program (see appendix F). I also assisted the administration with the management of athletics. I assisted with the scheduling of the gym, ordered equipment, communicated with the athletic directors at other schools regarding schedule changes, and coordinated pregame setup and organization of the gymnasium (see appendices B and Q). In addition, I managed my coaching programs by adhering to all aspects of school law, including timely recording of student injuries and carrying at all times copies of the student physical release forms (see appendix G).

As eighth-grade team leader, I am responsible for many duties, including setting, organizing, and leading meetings; scheduling new students and making schedule changes; contacting parents and coordinating parent conferences; communicating with the administration, social services personnel, teachers, parents, and students; and planning activities, classes, and schedules for the future. I also managed files on all students, organized mailings, and coordinated team meetings with students.

Teaching and Learning Philosophy

In teaching language arts, I use a variety of methods in order to meet the individual needs of every child. My methods include teacher-directed, student-directed, and cooperative groups, shared inquiry, and self-exploration. I integrate the many teaching methods so that I can perform as I believe a teacher should—as a facilitator. I believe that every child can be successful, and in order to be successful, each student must be actively involved in his or her learning. When I am acting as a facilitator, the students are able to take more accountability for and interest in their learning.

Motivating students is one way I help my students succeed. On a daily basis, students are encouraged to reach, and even go beyond, their potential. Writing activities challenge students to integrate research and reading and write at a high school level. Real-life situations and hands-on activities like working with a group of peers, giving oral presentations, designing advertisements, and publishing newspapers motivate students, as they are meaningful tasks that they may encounter throughout their lives (see appendices H and I). I also believe that recognizing the achievements of the students is an excellent form of motivation (see appendix J).

Effective communication and interaction with parents and the community is also an important aspect of my teaching philosophy. I believe that the education of every child is important to the entire community because an educated child is a productive child who will function as a good citizen. I communicate with parents on a regular basis via phone calls, letters home, and a personal web page (see appendices E and J).

To help the students further their education, I monitor their progress closely, share their progress with them frequently, and develop plans with them to improve their education. I monitor and communicate with students in many ways, including individual conferences, positive phone calls and notes home, and weekly progress reports. In addition, I keep my students' grades on a computerized grade book, and I teach the students how to use the program; when there is time during class, lunch, or homeroom, students are free to go to the computer and check their grades and assignments. I believe this is an important aspect of keeping my classroom centered on the students and their individual progress (see appendices D and J).

Teaching Responsibilities

During my seven years of teaching in public school, I have taught a variety of courses to seventh-grade and eighth-grade students. My primary teaching responsibility has been eighth grade language arts. I have taught the Virginia Standards of Learning to eighth-grade students in heterogeneous and homogeneous classroom environments. I have also served as cooperating teacher in the area of language arts for practicum students from area colleges, the most recent being from James Madison University (see appendix A).

In addition to language arts, I have taught math 8, Literacy Passport remediation/tutoring, drama, and creative arts. As an eighth-grade math teacher, I taught the Virginia Standards of Learning to average and below-average students in a heterogeneously grouped setting. My responsibilities as a drama teacher included teaching students in seventh and eighth grade the basics of drama and directing the school musical (see appendix P). To support the reading and writing resource teachers, I have tutored students in grades seven and eight who need to retake the Literacy Passport Test. I also taught a creative arts class that focused on visual and performing arts. One of the primary focuses of this class was creating public service messages to air on the local television station (see appendix P).

I have also served my county as a basketball, tennis, and track coach. As I do teach the fundamentals of basketball, tennis, and long-distance running, I consider this one of my teaching responsibilities. I also consider my coaching an important part of my teaching responsibilities because I teach the athletes the importance of hard work, goal setting, sportsmanship, teamwork, and respect.

Assessment of Effectiveness

I believe my leadership practices have been effective. My classroom is an enjoyable environment that students look forward to entering. Team meetings and committee meetings that I lead are positive and not looked on as just another boring, time-consuming drudgery. I have the support and respect of my colleagues, my students, and my students' parents and have taken great pride in my leadership and educational skills. My colleagues in my building are complimentary of the high educational standards I set, the students' parents support and respect me, and the English teachers at the high school commend me for doing an excellent job of preparing students for their high school experiences (see appendices E, N, and 0).

Improvement Activities

Over the past seven years I have attended many conferences and workshops in a variety of areas. This past summer, I attended an English Vertical Teaming conference. As a result of this conference, I enhanced my ability to work closely with the high school, assisted with the development of the first English concept to be taught in a strand from grades seven through twelve, and conducted workshops to instruct other teachers in my county about this teaming process (see appendices A and M).

During my first few years of teaching, I participated in a two-year research project for Appalachia Educational Laboratory (AEL) with seven other teachers and an administrator. After developing a schoolwide interdisciplinary unit, implementing the unit, and gathering research, our team drafted a document that was later published by AEL. I also participated in a weekend publishing institute with AEL in which a team of teachers drafted a publication of interdisciplinary units and projects (see appendices L and M).

In 1993 and 1994, I was a presenter at the Virginia Middle School Association Conference. In 1993 I presented (with a colleague) an interdisciplinary unit on *The Diary of Anne Frank*. In 1994 I presented a unit on newspaper skills (see appendix K).

Throughout my seven years of teaching, I have taken several mathematics courses. In 1992 I attended a seminar entitled

"Applications of Mathematics." In 1997 I took two math courses through UVA, "Teaching and Learning Algebra: Meeting the Challenges of 'Algebra for Everyone'" and a course in teaching the new Virginia Standards of Learning (see appendix M).

In the fall of 1997, I taught myself to use a new computerized grade book system and instructed other faculty members in my building in the use of the program. In addition, I have attended a conference on strengthening reading comprehension (presented by Roger Faff), received training as a small-group facilitator from Shalom et Benedictus in Winchester, and attended a forum titled "Understanding and Managing the Aggressive and Challenging Behaviors of Children and Youth" at James Madison University (see appendices D and M). I am currently enrolled in the Leadership Academy at George Mason University. This personal development will continue through the summer of 2000.

Future Administrative Goals

I plan to finish my educational leadership degree through George Mason University by the summer of 2000. After completing classes, I plan to complete my internship, take the praxis, and begin interviewing for a position as an assistant principal in a middle or high school. It is my hope to eventually achieve a position as a principal; I have enjoyed my years of teaching and hope that I can make an even greater impact in this leadership role.

George Kornegay
High School Leadership Portfolio Narrative

Table of Contents

Narrative
Appendices

Teaching Responsibilities

As an English teacher for ten years, I have taught a variety of high school English courses on the full range of ability levels. My primary teaching responsibilities have been with eleventh-graders enrolled in American literature courses. I have taught basic, average, college preparatory, and honors American literature classes. I have also taught remedial freshman English and advanced placement senior English. I have taught classes ranging in size from nine to thirty-five.

In addition to traditional English courses, I have also taught journalism and mass media. In journalism, I taught students the basics of newspaper reporting, layout, and design. My students published school newspapers and the yearbook, both of which received several awards at state competition.

I implemented the mass media technology program at Thomas County Central High School. Students enrolled in mass media technology produce a daily television program reporting school news. The class also produces a number of videotapes each year for special programs. Videotapes produced by the mass media technology class have won district, state, and national recognition.

Courses taught include:

Honors Junior English: A survey of American authors from the colonial period to the present forms the core of the course, which also emphasizes composition skills, vocabulary development, and the research paper.

Advanced Placement English: AP English exposes students to a wide selection of world literature as they prepare for the AP English exam administered by the College Board. Students may earn up to fifteen hours of college credit through AP English.

Basic Junior English: This course utilizes works by American authors to teach basic reading and comprehension skills outlined in Georgia's Quality Core Curriculum. Composition skills and library skills are also addressed.

Mass Media Technology: Students learn the basics of news reporting as they gather and report school news and conduct on-camera interviews. Students also utilize editing equipment to produce a daily television program and other special video features.

Administrative Responsibilities

In 1992, I became chairman of the English department. As department chairman, I was responsible for administering the department's budget of $12,000. I also worked with the teachers in the department and with the administration in designing the departmental master schedule each summer. To establish a degree of consistency within the department, I led a group of teachers in developing a departmental handbook that outlines an articulated reading program, the departmental writing program, and the departmental grading system. A copy of the English department handbook is included in appendix A.

In the fall of 1994, the death of an assistant principal resulted in an unanticipated opening. I assumed this position on an interim basis in September 1994. My responsibilities include evaluating teachers using GTEP, administering the school's disciplinary and attendance policies, and securing substitute teachers as needed. I also work with club advisors in organizing the school's extracurricular activities. I approve club activities and fund-raisers and maintain the school calendar.

Teaching and Learning Philosophy

In teaching English, I rely on a combination of techniques including lecture, discussion, cooperative learning groups, individual and group projects, and compositions (see appendix J). No technique is appropriate for every teaching situation; therefore, it is important that one select the technique best suited to the content and the learner or learners. I place a heavy emphasis on writing as an instructional strategy since I believe in the research that shows that writing is a highly effective learning mode (see the writing across the curriculum program in appendix A).

I organize my curriculum into instructional units. Within each unit, there are opportunities for group work as well as individual work. Believing in a high degree of accountability, I give frequent quizzes. Each unit includes several opportunities for students to write about what they are learning.

I became an English teacher because of my appreciation for good literature. I try to share my enthusiasm for the subject in the hope that my enthusiasm will spark greater student interest.

Leadership Philosophy and Practices

Administrators have two primary tasks: showing consideration for subordinates and initiating the structure needed to accomplish the organization's mission. In providing leadership for others, I try to be very well-organized and predictable. Others know what to expect from me and can anticipate what I expect from them. I try to be the hardest working member of my department because I believe leading by example is the best way to make a positive difference.

Others accept structure more readily when they understand the rationale behind it. Therefore, I try to explain what needs to be accomplished and why it is important. Incorporating the ideas of others is necessary for consensus building. I believe that leadership should be a team effort. As many people as possible should be involved in the decision-making process. Through membership on my school's leadership team, I have participated in the shared-governance process and feel that it benefits school administrators, teachers, and students.

Analysis of Methods, Strategies

Technology has given teachers a number of new tools to use in the instructional process. CD-ROM computer research tools have revolutionized the teaching of the research paper. Over the course of the last ten years, I have tried to constantly revise my strategies and assignments to stay current with new technology. On-line computer searching capabilities that can be carried out from the English classroom have enabled students to include a wider variety of sources in their papers. Footnotes at the bottom of the page have given way to parenthetical citations, and the meticulous typing instructions have given way to the word processor. Clearly, one's strategies must be constantly evaluated and updated.

Believing that writing is an essential skill for all students, I stress the writing process in all of my classes. I encourage students to do prewriting activities, write, revise, edit, and rewrite as many times as is necessary to produce a quality product. I make myself available after school and before school to tutor students as needed. Students have my home phone number, and I have spent countless hours tutoring students at night on the telephone. Students know that I want them to succeed, and this encourages them to work harder.

Students in my mass media production classes produce detailed storyboards for their video productions. We then film, edit, and present their work. Students take great pride in their work when they know that they have a real audience. An example storyboard is included in appendix N.

When students are writing their formal research papers in the spring, I try to plan an informal "writing conference" with each student during the outlining stage. This gives me an opportunity to give a student advice about the direction of his or her paper before the student invests too much time in writing the first draft. I use standardized evaluation forms on all major writing assignments. These forms help me be certain that I stay consistent with expectations. Since students are provided with copies of the forms in advance, they are able to see exactly how they will be evaluated. This helps reduce student anxiety.

One activity that I developed is in use in several high schools across South Georgia. It is an essay revision-analysis activity that leads students through a series of specific exercises to help them improve the quality of their writing. This activity has helped make the revision step of the writing process more meaningful for my students and for students of other teachers who have adopted the activity. A copy of the activity is included in appendix J.

Representative Course Syllabi Including Assignments, Examinations, and Readings

At the beginning of each school year, I issue a syllabus in each class. The syllabus includes a narrative description of the course, a list of major instructional objectives, a list of texts and other readings, an outline of the content, class rules and regulations, course requirements, and the grading system. Sample copies of my course syllabi are included in appendix J. The syllabus helps facilitate communication between the teacher and students and between the teacher and parents. It also serves as an outline to help provide a flexible but consistent pace for the school year. When I digress from the syllabus, it is intentional and with proper notification to students.

Awards and Recognitions

Louis B. Newton Medallion of Academic Excellence, Awarded by Mercer University upon receipt of B.A. degrees in English and Christianity in June 1985. Mercer presents the Newton medal

each spring quarter to the graduate who has exhibited the
highest academic achievement in that year's graduating class.

Outstanding Teacher Awards presented by the Burke County Board
of Education, Spring 1986, 1987, and 1988

STAR teacher awards 1988 and 1991

Central High School and Thomas County Teacher of the Year, 1990

Achievements earned by my students

1987:   Coached the region champion debate team
1990:   Won state honors for yearbook and newspaper
1991:   Won state honors for yearbook and newspaper
1991:   Student won district-level essay competition
1992:   Won state honors for yearbook, newspaper, and television
         production
1992:   Student won district-level essay competition
1993:   Won state honors for yearbook, newspaper, and television
         production
1993:   Student won district level essay competition
1994:   Won state honors for newspaper and television production

Improvement Activities

I have constantly sought to improve the quality of my instruction and to
share my successes with others. Consequently, I have attended numerous
staff development programs and have conducted or helped to conduct
several others.

Staff Development Activities/Workshops Attended

Writing Is Thorough and Efficient (Project WrITE) (staff
development activity, 1985)

Data collection training for TPAI (staff development, Fall 1986)

Writing to Win (staff development, Fall, 1988)

Test-writing workshop (staff development, Fall 1989)

School improvement planning (staff development, Summer 1991)

Teaching critical thinking skills (Summer 1992)

Strategies to improve achievement in English/language arts (staff
development, Summer 1992)

Diffusing Verbal Aggression (Summer 1993)
Graphics and special effects for television (Workshop, Summer 1993)

Staff Development Activities/Workshops Conducted

Producing Educational Videotapes, National School Boards Association Convention, Anaheim, California, March 1993
Producing Educational Videotapes, Georgia Association of Educational Leaders Convention, Jekyll Island, July 1993
Project WrITE staff development, Burke County School System, Summer 1986

Future Administrative Goals/Directions

Since I was in high school, I have had the goal of becoming a high school principal. Because I believe that the principal's role as instructional leader of his or her school is foremost among his or her responsibilities, I sought extensive experience in the classroom before entering the field of administration. I have planned my career to roughly follow this plan: ten years in the classroom; ten years as an assistant principal; and ten years as the principal of a high school.

Since I am now in my tenth year as a teacher, I am ready to move to the second major step in my career plan. During the first ten years, I have served on the school leadership team, as department chair, and as a member of the school improvement team. As an assistant principal, I hope to serve under a dynamic building principal who can act as my mentor and can help prepare me for my own principalship someday.

Leadership Portfolio Evaluation Criteria

Intern _____ Date _____

University Supervisor _____ Advisor_____

Evaluator _____

On a scale of 1 to 5 (5 being high), how successfully does the work in this portfolio meet the following criteria?

1. Evidence provided on competency completion	1	2	3	4	5
2. Well-organized	1	2	3	4	5
3. Includes appropriate information on school improvement project	1	2	3	4	5
4. Includes a variety of work (forms, memos, agendas, etc.)	1	2	3	4	5
5. Shows clarity of writing	1	2	3	4	5
6. Shows conciseness of writing	1	2	3	4	5
7. Uses correct grammar	1	2	3	4	5
8. Is persuasive	1	2	3	4	5
9. Uses correct spelling	1	2	3	4	5
10. Looks neat and professional	1	2	3	4	5
11. Materials are current	1	2	3	4	5
12. Supportive evidence for narrative is provided	1	2	3	4	5

Comments _____

_____

_____

~~~ References

Advanced programs in educational leadership for principals, superintendents, curriculum directors, and supervisors. (1995). Washington, DC: National Council for Accreditation for Teacher Education (prepared by the National Policy Board for Educational Administration).

American Association for School Administrators. (1982). *Guidelines for the preparation of school administrators.* Arlington, VA: Author.

American Association of Colleges for Teacher Education. (1988). *School leadership preparation: A preface for action.* Washington, DC: Author.

Bacharach, S. B. (Ed.). (1990). *Educational reform. Making sense of it all.* Boston: Allyn and Bacon.

Bennett, K. (1993). Coaching for leadership: Moving toward site-based management. *NASSP Bulletin, 77*(552), 81–91.

Bensimon, E. M., & Neumann, A. (1993). *Redesigning collegiate leadership: Teams and teamwork in higher education.* Baltimore: Johns Hopkins University Press.

Bridges, E. M. (1991). *Problem based learning for administrators.* Eugene, OR: ERIC Clearinghouse on Educational Management, University of Oregon.

Brown, G., & Irby, B. J. (1997). The principal portfolio. Thousand Oaks, CA: Corwin Press.

Bush, G. (1991). *America 2000: An education strategy.* Washington, DC: U.S. Department of Education.

Campbell, R. F., Fleming, T., Newell, L. J., & Bennion, J. W. (1987). *A history of thought and practice in educational administration.* New York: Teachers College Press.

A capsule description of selected factors at Valdosta State College: A key component of a proposed South Georgia regional university. (1989). Valdosta, GA: Valdosta State College.

Chance, E. E., & Grady, M. L. (1990). Creating and implementing a vision for the school. *NASSP Bulletin, 74*(529), 12–18.

Cutlip, S., Center, A., & Bloom, J. (1985). *Effective public relations.* Englewood Cliffs, NJ: Prentice-Hall.

Dewey, J. (1981). Experience and nature. In J. Boydston (Ed.), *John Dewey: The later works, 1925–1953* (pp. 266–294). Carbondale, IL: Southern Illinois Press. (Original work published 1925)

Edgerton, R., Hutchings, P., & Quinlan, K. (1991). *The teaching portfolio: Capturing the scholarship in teaching.* Washington, DC: American Association for Higher Education.

Education personnel preparation and certification rules and procedures. (2001). Atlanta: Georgia Professional Standards Commission.

Elam, S. M., Rose, L. C., & Gallup, A. M. (1994). The 26th annual Phi Delta Kappa/Gallup Poll of the public's attitudes toward the public schools. *Phi Delta Kappa, 76*(1), 41–56.

Frye, B. J. (Ed.) (1994). *Teaching in college* (3rd ed.). Cleveland, OH: InfoTec.

Georgia teacher certification tests: Field 23: Administration and supervision. (1988). Atlanta: Georgia Department of Education.

Griffiths, D. E. (1988). Administrative theory. In N. J. Boyan (Ed.), *Handbook of research on educational administration,* (pp. 27–51). New York: Longman.

Griffiths, D. E., Stout, R. T., & Forsyth, P. B. (1988). *Leaders for America's schools.* Berkeley, CA: McCutchan.

Hallinger, P., & Murphy, J. (1991). Developing leaders for tomorrow's schools. *Phi Delta Kappan, 72*(7), 514–520.

Hanson, E. M. (1991). *Educational administration and organizational behavior* (3rd ed.). Boston: Allyn and Bacon.

Harvey, T., & Brolet, B. (1994). *Building teams: Building people.* Lancaster, PA: Technomic.

Hoy, W. K., & Miskel, C. G. (1991). *Educational administration: Theory, research, practice* (4th ed.). New York: McGraw-Hill.

Jackson, P. (1986). How to build public relationships that motivate real support. *NASSP Bulletin, 70,* 25–31.

Kirby, P. C., & Colbert, R. (1994). Principals who empower teachers. *Journal of School Leadership,* 4(1), 39–49.

Leadership performance assessment instrument (pilot draft). (1987). Atlanta: Georgia Department of Education.

Leithwood, K. A. (1992). The move toward transformational leadership. *Educational Leadership,* 49(5), 8–12.

McKeachie, W. J. (Ed.) (1994). *Teaching tips: Strategies, research, and theory for college and university teachers* (9th ed.). Lexington, MA: D. C. Heath.

McKernan, J. R., Jr. (1994). *The national education goals report: Building a nation of learners.* Washington, DC: U.S. Government Printing Office.

Midgley, C., & Wood, S. (1993). Beyond site-based management: Empowering teachers to reform schools. *Phi Delta Kappan,* 75(3), 245–252.

Milstein, M. M., & Associates (1993). *Changing the way we prepare educational leaders.* Newbury Park, CA: Corwin Press.

Morgan, P. L. (1995, August). *The internship: Theory to practice.* Paper presented at the annual conference of the National Council of Professors of Educational Administration, Williamsburg, VA.

Murphy, J. (Ed.). (1993a). Ferment in school administration. In J. Murphy (Ed.), *Preparing tomorrow's school leaders: Alternative designs.* University Park, PA: University Council for Educational Administration.

Murphy, J. (Ed.). (1993b). *Preparing tomorrow's school leaders: Alternative designs.* University Park, PA: University Council for Educational Administration.

A nation at risk: The imperative for educational reform. (1993). Washington, DC: National Council for Accreditation for Teacher Education.

National Association of Elementary School Principals. (1990). *Principals for 21st century schools.* Alexandria, VA: Author.

National Association of Secondary School Principals. (1985). *Performance-based preparation of principals.* Reston, VA: Author.

National Association of Secondary School Principals. (1992). *Developing school leaders: A call for collaboration.*. Reston, VA: Author.

NCATE refined standards. (1994). Washington, DC: National Council for Accreditation of Teacher Education.

Norton, D. J. (1990, October 23). *Valdosta State College master's level program in administration and supervision is administratively approved until the next on-site review.* Atlanta: Georgia Department of Education.

Peper, J. B. (1988). Clinical education for school superintendents and principals: The missing link. In D. E. Griffiths, R. T. Stout, & P. B. Forsyth (Eds.), *Leaders for America schools.* Berkeley, CA: McCutchan.

Principals for our changing schools: Knowledge and skill base (1993). Fairfax, VA: National Policy Board for Educational Administration.

Quality basic education act of Georgia. (1984). Atlanta: Georgia Department of Education.

Report of NCATE reaccreditation visit of Valdosta State College. (1989, November 15). Charlottesville: University of Virginia Board of Examiners.

Richards, J. J., & Fox, A. (1990). The internship: A meaningful experience for new administrators. *NASSP Bulletin, 74*(526), 26–28.

Robbins, P. (1991). *How to plan and implement a peer coaching program.* Alexandria, VA: Association for Supervision and Curriculum Development.Sagor, R. (1992). *How to conduct collaborative action research.* Alexandria, VA: Association for Supervision and Curriculum Development.

Schlechty, P. C. (1990). *Schools for the 21st century.* San Francisco, CA: Jossey-Bass.

Schon, D. A. (1987). *Educating the reflective practitioner.* San Francisco, CA: Jossey-Bass.

Seldin, P. (1993). *Successful use of teaching portfolios.* Bolton, MA: Anker.

Standards for the accreditation of teacher education. (1982). Washington, DC: National Council for Accreditation of Teacher Education.

Thomson, S. D., et al. (1993). *Principals for our changing schools: The knowledge and skill base.* Fairfax, VA: National Policy Board for Educational Administration.

Toffler, A. (1980). *The third wave.* New York: William Morrow.

Tozer, S. E., Violas, P. D., & Senese, G. B. (1995). *School and society: Historical and contemporary perspectives* (2nd ed.). New York: McGraw-Hill.

University Council for Education Administration. (1987). *Leaders for America's schools: The report of the National Commission on Excellence in Educational Administration.* Tempe, AZ: Author.

Walker, P. A., & Roder, L. R. (1993). Reflections on school-based management and teacher empowerment. *Journal of Law and Education, 22*(2), 159–175.

Watkins, B. T. (1989, October 4). Denials of reaccreditation rise sharply under new teacher education policies. *Chronicle of Higher Education,* 36, A13–A14.

Wylie, V. L. (Ed.). (1988–1989). *Creating visionary leaders: Knowledge base document.* Unpublished report prepared by the faculty of the Department of Educational Administration and Supervision during self-study in preparation for National Council of Accreditation of Teacher Education (NCATE) visit November 12–15, 1989. Valdosta, GA: School of Education.

Wylie, V. L., & Clark, E. H. (1992). Evaluation of rigor and value as a base for restructuring the administrative internship. In F. C. Wendel (Ed.), *Reforming administrator preparation programs* (pp. 57–69). University Park, PA: University Council for Educational Administration.

Wylie, V. L., & Clark, E. H. (1994). Personal observation of using peer coaching to improve the administrative internship. *Journal of School Leadership, 4*(5), 543–556.

Wylie, V. L., & Michael, R. O. (1989, October). *The knowledge base in educational administration: Serving many masters.* Paper presented at the annual convention of The University Council for Educational Administration, Paradise Valley, AZ.

Wylie, V. L., & Michael, R. O. (1990). School reform in Georgia: Who will bell the cat? *GATEways to Teacher Education, 3*(1), 1–9.

Index

◀ About the Authors

P. Lená Morgan received an Ed.D. degree in educational leadership from Auburn University and M.S. degree in educational administration from Florida State University. Currently, she is the dean of curriculum implementation at Pensacola Junior College. Prior to moving into higher education, she served as a middle school and high school teacher, building-level administrator, and central office administrator. In addition to serving as a department head in educational leadership, Dr. Morgan has taught M.Ed., Ed.S., and doctoral-level administration and research courses as Valdosta State University, George Mason University, and the State University of West Georgia. It was while working at Valdosta State University that she worked with the other authors in developing effective internship experiences for their masters and doctoral students. Her primary research efforts focus on developing a seamless transition from preschool through college and on working with difficult children in the traditional classroom. She has collaborated on numerous journal articles, has coauthored three books, and has presented at numerous conferences and workshops.

C. Jay Hertzog (B.S., M.Ed., and Ed.D., the Pennsylvania State University), a former teacher, middle level assistant principal and principal, and assistant superintendent, is the dean of education at Slippery Rock University in Pennsylvania. A former postdoctoral student with Dr. Alfred Arth, he is a past member of NMSA's board of trustees and cofounder (with John Lounsbury) of the National Professors of Middle Level Education (NaPOMLE). He entered the field of higher education at Valdosta State University in Georgia, where he taught middle level education courses, later moving to the department of educational leadership. It was in this department that he worked with the other authors in developing effective internship experiences for their masters and doctoral students. In addition, he and Dr. Lená Morgan have conducted research on the transition from elementary school to middle school and middle to high. school. They have collaborated on numerous articles dealing with the effects of transition as students move into and out of middle school. They have presented at both state and national conferences and have worked with schools across the country in developing programs to help students succeed.

Albert S. Gibbs (B.S. and M.S., Central Connecticut State College; Ed.S., University of Connecticut; and Ph.D., Georgia State University, in educational leadership) is a professor of educational leadership, a department head for early childhood and reading education, and a full member of the graduate faculty and doctoral faculty at Valdosta State University. Dr. Gibbs was an elementary teach for eight years and an elementary principal for fourteen years. He has coauthored one text on the internship for educational leaders, published several articles in scholarly journals, and has presented numerous papers and symposia at scholarly conferences. His current interest is in improving the preparation of early childhood teachers and developing principals as instructional leaders. His current research focuses on the academic preparation, teaching backgrounds, certification types and levels, and career paths of elementary school principals.